Lean
Italian Cooking

Also by Anne Casale
Published by Ballantine Books

Italian Family Cooking

The Long Life Cookbook

Lean Italian Cooking

Anne Casale

Foreword by Lynne S. Hill, M.S., R.D.

FAWCETT COLUMBINE • NEW YORK

Library of Congress Cataloging-in-Publication Data
Casale, Anne.
Lean Italian Cooking / Anne Casale.—1st ed.
        p.   cm.
Includes index.
ISBN 0-449-90788-0
1. Cookery, Italian.   2. Low-fat diet—Recipes.   3. Low-cholesterol diet—
Recipes.   I. Title.
TX723.C2973   1994
641.5945—dc20   93-4964
                                                                                    CIP

Designed by Ann Gold
Manufactured in the United States of America

First Edition: February 1994

10   9   8   7   6   5

To my two wonderful daughters, Joanne and Amy,
both talented artists and both excellent cooks,
who learned the true values of home cooking at an
early age in our kitchen and have carried the
true love of their heritage into their homes.

My love to you, Joanne and Amy, who have always
been my pride, joy, and inspiration.

ACKNOWLEDGMENTS

Sincere thanks to my literary agent, Amy Berkower, who after hearing of the strong reaction to the lean Italian cooking courses I had been teaching, responded with enthusiasm and gusto, "That's your next book, Annie."

My personal thanks to Lynne Hill, M.S., R.D., for her professional nutritional analysis of my recipes.

My biggest thank-you once again to David Wald, a very dear friend, for the many hours spent helping me put my thoughts into words.

Contents

Vegetables

Salads

Cookies

Nutrition and Lean Italian Cooking

※

s a registered dietitian, I have witnessed with enthusiasm the recent transition from excess to moderation in the American diet. Experts in chronic diseases have shown convincing links between diet and coronary heart disease, strokes, diabetes mellitus, and certain cancers. Now we are told that we must change our eating patterns in order to lower our risk of these diseases, decreasing our intake of fats, meats, sugar, and sodium in particular.

However, obsessive concern with these strictures threatens to drain the pleasure from cooking and dining. In the United States, a whole new industry has sprung up to reformulate familiar foods and to develop replacements for sugar, salt, and fats. The food experience can now easily be reduced to frantic label-reading and the consumption of bland, synthetic meals—an anxiety-ridden chore. We need a new approach.

In certain areas of the world, the occurrence of food-related chronic diseases is much lower than it is in the United States. Italy and other Mediterranean countries, thanks to their traditional approach to meal-planning, are among these areas. Relatively small amounts of meat, poultry, and dairy products are supplemented by abundant fruits, vegetables, and grains, with their vibrant colors and varied textures; herbs and spices add sprightly flavor. Olive oil, high in healthful monounsaturated fats, replaces to a large degree the saturated fats in butter, lard, and cream favored by other cuisines. Eating in these countries is a joy unclouded by guilt.

Anne Casale, in *Lean Italian Cooking*, presents a delightful collection of traditional dishes that she has made even lighter in cal-

~~~~~~

ories and fats, accomplishing what many other cooks have been trying to do for years. Anne's recipes adhere to modern scientific recommendations with no loss of ethnic authenticity. She has captured the essence of Italian cooking through moderation, not deprivation, calling on her forty years of cooking and teaching experience to bring us healthful Italian fare. If the concept of good nutrition makes your family shudder, treat them to these delicious dishes without comment. Their bodies will benefit even as their palates are delighted.

▦

Lean Italian Cooking is consistent with the new United States Department of Agriculture's Food Guide Pyramid, which emphasizes complex carbohydrates derived from grains, fruits, and vegetables. Meats, fish, poultry, and low-fat dairy products are recommended in moderate amounts, while quantities of fats and simple sugars are kept low. Foods in each grouping are approximately equal in nutritional value, and may be exchanged within the group.

The concept of "servings" can be confusing. For example, ¾ ounce dry pasta counts as 1 serving. If a recipe allows 3 ounces of pasta per person, this makes 4 "servings," out of a total daily allowance of 6 to 11. Additionally, the range of "servings" for each food group encompasses individual differences. An inactive female would choose the lower suggested amounts, while an active man would select the higher number. In the food groupings discussed here, the recommended number of "servings" in each category is for one day.

Pyramid Food Groups and Suggested Servings

Bread, Cereal, Rice, and Pasta: The recommendation is 6 to 11 "servings." About ¾ ounce dry or ½ cup cooked pasta constitutes 1 serving. One slice of bread, ½ cup cooked rice, ½ cup cooked cereal or 1 ounce ready-to-eat cereal, 3 cups popcorn, 1 six-inch tortilla, ½ of a hamburger or hot dog bun are other servings. The

FOOD GUIDE PYRAMID

A GUIDE TO DAILY FOOD CHOICES

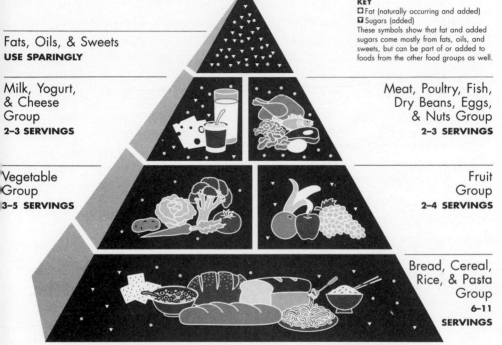

KEY
☐ Fat (naturally occurring and added)
▼ Sugars (added)
These symbols show that fat and added sugars come mostly from fats, oils, and sweets, but can be part of or added to foods from the other food groups as well.

Fats, Oils, & Sweets
USE SPARINGLY

Milk, Yogurt,
& Cheese
Group
2–3 SERVINGS

Meat, Poultry, Fish,
Dry Beans, Eggs,
& Nuts Group
2–3 SERVINGS

Vegetable
Group
3–5 SERVINGS

Fruit
Group
2–4 SERVINGS

Bread, Cereal,
Rice, & Pasta
Group
**6–11
SERVINGS**

SOURCE: U.S. Department of Agriculture/U.S. Department of Health and Human Services

Use the Food Guide Pyramid to help you eat better every day . . . the Dietary Guidelines way. Start with plenty of Breads, Cereals, Rice, and Pasta; Vegetables; and Fruits. Add two to three servings from the Milk group and two to three servings from the Meat group.

Each of these food groups provides some, but not all, of the nutrients you need. No one food group is more important than another—for good health you need them all. Go easy on fats, oils, and sweets, the foods in the small tip of the Pyramid.

low-fat focaccias and pizzas, as well as polenta, are also examples of foods in this grouping.

Vegetables: The recommendation is 3 to 5 "servings." A cup of raw leafy vegetables or ½ cup of cooked or chopped nonleafy vegetables counts as a serving. Vegetables are low in calories, almost fat-free, and an excellent source of fiber, vitamins, and minerals.

Vegetables play a large role in Italian cuisine. Included in this collection are recipes for them as side dishes and salads, but also as a part of soups, entrées, polenta, and rice, and as toppings for pizza and focaccia.

Fruits: The recommendation is 2 to 4 "servings." A medium apple, orange, or banana, ½ cup cooked or canned fruit, or ¾ cup juice counts as a serving.

Italians frequently enjoy fresh fruit as dessert. You will find delicious cooked fruit preparations here for those times when you want a more complex dessert.

Meat, Poultry, Fish, Dry Beans, Eggs, and Nuts: The recommendation is 2 or 3 "servings" per day. This group is the primary source of protein, and provides many vitamins and minerals as well. Recommended amounts are limited to 2 or 3 ounces of lean meat, fish, or poultry; 2 or 3 eggs; 1½ cups cooked beans; 4 to 6 tablespoons peanut butter; and ⅔ to 1 cup nuts. If a higher fat protein source is chosen, use a low-fat choice the next meal.

In *Lean Italian Cooking* only the leanest cuts of meat are used. The skin is removed from poultry, and there is an ample offering of recipes using healthful seafood and fish.

Milk, Yogurt, and Cheese: The recommendation is 2 or 3 "servings." One cup of low-fat or skim milk or yogurt, 2 cups low-fat cottage cheese, and 1½ ounces of part-skim mozzarella or ricotta are each a serving.

~~~~~~

Using the low-fat versions of ricotta and mozzarella, and carefully measuring foods from this group, as directed in the recipes, will add flavor, creaminess, and calcium and protein to your diet while keeping calories and fat content moderate.

Fats, Oils, and Sugars: These make up the tiny top of the pyramid. They contribute flavor and smoothness to recipes, but since their basic contribution to nutrition is "empty" calories, they should be used only in small amounts.

The recipes in this book use small amounts of olive oil, which gives the flavor and cooking benefits of oil with fewer unhealthful aspects found in other fats.

Nutrition Information

The following information will help you to understand the nutrition analyses found in this book:

Calories (cal.)—a measure of energy in foods. It is recommended that you eat the number of calories that allow you to maintain "ideal body weight." Thus, appropriate daily caloric intake will vary from person to person.

Cholesterol (chol.) is found in foods from animal sources—meat, poultry, seafood, eggs, and dairy products. It is wise to keep your daily intake to 250 to 300 mg.

Fat: An excess of fat is thought to lead to many serious diseases. Current recommendations are to limit your fat calories in a day (not in any one particular food) to 30 percent. To find out how many grams of fat you may safely eat in a day, multiply your total caloric intake by .3 and then divide by 9. For example, if you eat 1800 calories a day:

1800 (calories) × .3 = 540 (calories from fat)
540 (calories) from fat) ÷ 9 (calories in a gram of fat) = 60 (grams of fat you can eat in a day)

Sodium (sod.) is found naturally in most foods. When eaten in excess, it can contribute to heart disease, high blood pressure, stroke, and kidney disease. Current recommendations limit a day's intake to 2400 mg. Salt is the most common contributor to high sodium levels. One teaspoon has about 2200 mg.

Gram and milligram (gm and mg) are measures of weight. Nutrients eaten in large amounts, such as protein and fat, are reported in grams. Nutrients eaten in smaller amounts, such as sodium and cholesterol, are reported in milligrams. There are 1000 milligrams in 1 gram.

All analyses have been rounded to the nearest whole number.

—Lynne S. Hill, M.S., R.D.

Introduction: Lean Italian Cooking

I have spent the last forty years in the kitchen—not just as a wife and mother preparing meals for her family and loved ones, but as an instructor, author, food consultant, and director of my own cooking school.

In recent years, there has been an overwhelming response to the classes I have offered under the umbrella "Lean Italian Cooking." These courses cover a wide range of Italian regions that closely trace my family heritage. From the fishing villages along the coast of Liguria we stop at the seaport city of Genoa for a succulent grilled tuna with orange mint dressing. Then up into the mountains of Santo Stefano to experience rustic, peasant-inspired focaccia, a flat bread studded with golden garlic and fresh rosemary. Next, on to Tuscany where we visit the picturesque walled city of Lucca for a wonderfully robust soup, ribollita (a beautiful marriage of vegetables, cannellini beans, and sage served with traditional toasted bread cubes, Parmesan cheese, and parsley). Side trips follow to a remote little mountaintop village, Stabiano, to sample creamy polenta with kale and kidney beans. Then off to Campania for a savory braised chicken stew simmered with tomatoes, wine, olives, and herbs, which captures the spirit of Naples. In every region along the way, the adventurous voyager discovers that pasta prevails.

The reaction to these courses is always the same. After clarifying measurements, terms, and techniques, the real question is then always asked: "How is it possible to capture the true flavor of Italian cooking and still keep it light?"

The answer to this question provides the main focus for this book—moderation, not deprivation. I had to shift my mental gears a bit so that I could translate old traditional dishes into a new style of cooking with a lighter touch. I found the trick was to experiment with different cooking methods, stripping away fat and calories wherever possible but making the old favorites taste the way I remembered them. After exploring several techniques, I discovered a variety of ways to streamline these recipes to keep all the rich flavors without all the unwanted calories. The key to starting on your way to healthier eating is to strive for moderation and balance. To achieve the best possible results, I offer the following basic guidelines for creating lean Italian cooking.

- Don't rely on artificial substitutes; nothing tastes like the real thing. Rather than employ mock products, pure olive oil, imported Parmesan cheese, salt, sugar, wines, and liqueurs can be used in moderation to enhance the flavor of these Italian classics. I urge you to follow measurements as written to guarantee optimum flavor.

- Three different types of olive oil are used throughout the book. For recipes that simply specify olive oil, look for the word *pure* on the label. When extra virgin oil is listed, it is recommended for the distinctive, fruity accent and enticing aroma it adds to that particular dish. For baking, use light olive oil because its subtle flavor will not mask the baked goods. Throughout the book, directions are given for cooking spray to be used for greasing pans and broiling racks. This aerosol product is available as olive oil or vegetable oil. They work equally well.

- For soups, pasta, risotto, or polenta dishes calling for Parmesan cheese, the imported variety (Parmigiano Reggiano) is best. It is made from cow's milk and is less salty than the pecorino-style cheese (romano), which is made from ewe's milk. For lasagne or cream sauces, use part-skimmed ricotta and low-fat mozzarella rather than the rich whole milk varieties. Remember, in using cheese, I repeat: Follow measurements as written.

- In seasoning with salt, I recommend using coarse salt (kosher salt) because it is pure, with no additives, so very little is needed for flavoring. For baking, use common table salt.

- Before sautéing several of the meat, poultry, or fish recipes, I give them a light coating of Gold Medal Wondra flour. This is an instantized all-purpose flour that pours like salt. It gives a much lighter coating than all-purpose flour for sautéing and also helps retain the natural juices.

- In selecting meats, try to use only the leanest cuts. These are now generally available and come trimmed, with just a very thin layer of fat, which should be removed before cooking. Italians are not big meat eaters as a rule. We would do well to follow their example. Simple, healthy techniques for preparing beef, veal, lamb, and pork appear in the meat chapter.

- While chicken is low in fat and cholesterol, turkey has even fewer calories. Turkey breast cutlets or fillets can be substituted in recipes calling for veal scallops. One of my favorite recipes substitutes ground turkey for ground beef in stuffed peppers. Many recipes call for boneless skinless chicken breasts. Quickly sautéed or lightly grilled, delicately flavored with wine, herbs, and vegetables—ready in a matter of minutes for today's health-conscious yet slightly harried cook.

- The nutritional advantages of fish and seafood are widely recognized. Too often, these otherwise virtuous foods are deep-fried or drenched with sinful sauces. Not so here, where a multitude of techniques from grilling, braising, broiling, and roasting let the real flavor of the fish come through while retaining its rich texture the lean Italian way. These types of preparations lend themselves to the use of fresh herbs, vegetables, citrus juices, wines, and piquant vinegars to achieve vivacious seasonings.

- Vegetables are never treated as an afterthought or as an obligation, but as a major if not the principal part of an Italian meal. Many will be paired with pasta, risotto, and polenta dishes. Greens such as broccoli di rape, kale, escarole, spinach, and swiss chard, simply braised, are family favorites in many Italian households. No wonder their diet is one of the healthiest in the world.

- Salads, whether greens or vegetable, are usually served after the meal or as a second course when pasta, risotto, or polenta has been the main course. Dressing a salad takes more than a perfectly balanced vinaigrette. Fresh herbs such as parsley, mint, oregano, and chives make the difference in visual and taste impact, especially when the amount of oil used in the dressing has been decreased.

- People usually regard pizza and focaccia as fattening foods. Not so, especially when low-fat mozzarella cheese is used sparingly, and vegetables are used generously and creatively as toppings.

- Ending the meal with a delicious dessert doesn't have to mean loading up on fat and calories. Many Italian households serve fresh fruit at the end of a meal. While we know fruit is refreshing and low in calories, many of us still enjoy capping a meal with a more satisfying treat. Thanks to new methods of creating mousses, creams, and tortes, calories and fat can be shaved and flavor retained. Light cream cheese and low-fat milk can be blended to create fabulous nonfattening substitutes for heavy whipping cream. I offer improved methods for creating low-fat cookies and biscotti in the cookie chapter.

In cooking lean Italian, diverse and complementary tastes and textures are orchestrated to follow one another to create a harmonious whole. Quality is more important than quantity and, in fact, moderation is the critical element. Each dish is prepared in a direct, simple way. The balancing of different dishes within a meal provides enough complexity to create solid, satisfying food that is also lower in calories, cholesterol, fat, and sodium.

Mangia bene, an Italian expression meaning "eat well," is the toast I offer you. May *Lean Italian Cooking* allow you to cook lean and luscious meals for a longer, happier, healthier life.

Soups

Introduction

I have always loved to make and serve soups. To me, nothing is more homey or satisfying than such a full-bodied blending of ingredients slowly simmering on the stove. This feeling stems from my childhood, when soup was served for lunch, as a first course for dinner, or for dinner itself. Its versatility was limitless. Soup recipes offered in this chapter can serve as a satisfying lunch or first course. Many of the heartier soups, such as tuscan bean, winter vegetable, or yellow split-pea, may stand on their own as a substantial main course when accompanied by a simple tossed salad and hearty slices of Italian bread or foccacia.

The basis of any good soup is the broth. Broths are easy to make and can be kept in the freezer for months. They are also an essential ingredient for many of the recipes found in this book.

If you plan to use the broth within a week, it may be stored in wide-mouth jars in the refrigerator. Storing in a wide-mouth jar will make it easier to spoon off and discard any solidified surface fat from either chicken or beef broth.

For freezing, transfer broth to plastic containers, leaving 1½ inches of headspace to allow for expansion. This will simplify removal when ready to use. Run bottom of container under a little water and frozen broth will pop right out. Using a small paring knife, scrape away frozen surface fat before defrosting.

Broth can be frozen in ice cube trays for sauces, braised dishes, and stews. To do so, transfer 2½ cups broth to a 1-quart glass measuring cup. Carefully pour broth into a 16-section plastic ice cube tray. Freeze overnight. Run bottom of tray briefly under warm water before popping. Scrape away any surface fat from cubes. Transfer to plastic bags, seal tightly and store in freezer. Each cube is equivalent to 2 tablespoons broth. Broth can be frozen up to 4 months.

If you do not have the time to make broth, you may substitute a low-sodium canned broth, which is significantly less salty than either regular or reduced-sodium canned broth. For canned chicken broth, you can use low-sodium Campbell's, Pritikin, or Health Valley. For low-sodium beef broth, Health Valley is recommended. (Campbell's and Pritikin are available in most supermarkets; Health Valley may be purchased in health food stores). Whenever a recipe calls for vegetable broth, low-sodium canned chicken broth may be substituted if you have no homemade broth on hand.

Whether you choose to make your own or select a low-sodium canned variety of broth, soup is versatile, satisfying, irresistible, hearty, and healthy.

Beef Broth

[Brodo di Manzo]

⊞

2½ QUARTS

2½ pounds beef hind shank, cut into 3 cross cuts

1½ pounds beef bones

2 medium-size unpeeled yellow onions, quartered

4 medium-size carrots (10 ounces), trimmed, and cut into 2-inch pieces

3 stalks celery including leaves (6 ounces), cut into 2-inch pieces

2 teaspoons whole black peppercorns

3 large cloves garlic, unpeeled

1 large bay leaf

2 sprigs fresh thyme or ½ teaspoon dried thyme

10 sprigs Italian flat-leaf parsley

1 cup canned whole, peeled tomatoes, coarsely chopped, including juice

1. Adjust oven rack to center of oven and preheat to 475°F.

2. In a large roasting pan, place beef shanks and bones. Place onions, carrots, and celery in between meat and bones and roast until meat and bones are well browned on both sides, turning once, about 30 minutes. Transfer meat and bones to a 10-quart pot, leaving vegetables in pan.

3. Add 2 cups water to roasting pan. Bring to a boil over high heat, scraping up any fragments of meat and vegetables that cling to bottom and sides of pan with wooden spoon. Transfer vegetables to pot. Add peppercorns, garlic, bay leaf, thyme, and parsley.

4. Add 3 quarts of cold water to pot (or enough water to cover meat and vegetable mixture by 2 inches). Bring to a boil over medium-low heat, partially covered. Using a skimmer or small strainer, skim off the froth as it collects on the surface while the water comes to a boil. Turn heat to low and simmer, partially covered, for 2 hours. Add chopped tomatoes and cook for an additional 30 minutes. Turn heat off, cover pot, and let broth rest for at least 2 hours before straining.

5. Using a pair of tongs, transfer meat to platter and reserve for sandwiches. Remove bones and discard. Strain broth through a fine

mesh strainer lined with a double thickness of dampened cheese-cloth into another pot, squeezing cheesecloth after straining to extract as much liquid as possible. Discard remaining solids. Cool broth to room temperature and pour into jars with tight-fitting lids. Broth may be kept in refrigerator for 1 week, or frozen in plastic containers or ice cube trays for up to 4 months (see page 2 for storing method). When ready to use, discard solidified fat from surface.

PER CUP: Cal. 24   Chol. 0 mg
            Fat .47 gm   Sod. 50 mg

Chicken Broth

[Brodo di Pollo]

3 QUARTS

4   pounds chicken parts, such as necks, backs, and wings, thoroughly washed in cold water
1   large yellow onion (10 ounces), peeled and quartered
3   stalks celery including leaves (6 ounces), cut into 2-inch chunks
2   large carrots (7 ounces), trimmed, and cut into 2-inch pieces
10 sprigs Italian flat-leaf parsley
3   large cloves garlic, unpeeled
1   teaspoon whole black peppercorns

1. Place chicken parts in a 10-quart pot. Add about 4 quarts cold water (or enough water to cover chicken parts by 3 inches). Slowly bring to a boil, partially covered, over low heat. Using a skimmer or small strainer, skim off the froth as it collects on the surface while the water comes to a boil. Repeat skimming 2 or 3 times until there is very little froth left floating on top. Add remaining ingredients and continue simmering, partially covered,

over low heat for 2 hours. Turn off heat, cover pot, and let broth rest for at least 2 hours before straining.

2. Strain broth through a fine mesh strainer lined with a double thickness of dampened cheesecloth into another pot, squeezing cheesecloth after straining broth to extract as much liquid as possible. Discard the solids. Cool broth to room temperature and pour into jars with tight-fitting lids. Broth may be kept in refrigerator for 1 week, or frozen in plastic containers or ice cube trays up to 4 months (see page 2 for storing method). When ready to use, discard solidified fat from surface.

PER CUP: Cal. 26   Chol. 0 mg
          Fat 1 gm   Sod. 42 mg

Vegetable Broth
[Brodo di Legumi]

3 QUARTS

1 large Spanish onion (10 ounces), peeled, quartered, and cut into 1-inch chunks

4 carrots (1 pound), trimmed, and coarsely chopped

6 stalks celery including leaves (12 ounces), cut into 2-inch lengths

4 large plum tomatoes (1 pound), halved, cored, quartered, and cut into 1-inch chunks

8 large mushrooms (8 ounces), thickly sliced

6 large cloves garlic, unpeeled

10 sprigs Italian flat-leaf parsley

10 short sprigs fresh thyme or 1 tablespoon dried thyme

2 bay leaves

1 tablespoon whole black peppercorns

1. Place all of the ingredients in an 8-quart pot and cover with 5 quarts of cold water. Bring to a boil over high heat. Lower heat

and simmer, partially covered, for 2½ hours. Remove from heat and let broth rest for 1 hour.

2. Strain broth through a fine mesh strainer lined with a double thickness of dampened cheesecloth into another pot. Press on solids with the back of a large spoon as you strain. Discard remaining solids.

3. Cool broth to room temperature and pour into jars with tight-fitting lids. Broth can be kept in refrigerator for 1 week, or can be frozen in plastic containers or ice cube trays for up to 4 months (see page 2 for storing method).

PER CUP: Cal. 21   Chol. 0 mg
            Fat .18 gm   Sod. 19 mg

Broccoli Soup with Tubettini

[Zuppa di Broccoli]

MAKES 9 CUPS, SERVES 6

Tubettini, tiny tubular pasta, and broccoli are cooked together to create a light, nourishing soup that can be prepared in less than 30 minutes.

1   large bunch broccoli
    (about 1½ pounds)
1   tablespoon olive oil
½   cup minced red onion
½   cup minced celery, strings
    removed before mincing
5½ cups Chicken Broth,
    preferably homemade
    (page 5), or defatted low-
    sodium canned

1   tablespoon minced fresh
    sage or 1 teaspoon
    crumbled dried sage
½   teaspoon coarse salt
¼   teaspoon crushed red pepper
    flakes
½   cup tubettini (tiny tubular
    pasta)
2   tablespoons freshly grated
    imported Parmesan
    cheese, for serving

1. Remove florets from broccoli, leaving about ½ inch of their stems. Cut florets into ½-inch pieces. Wash in cold water, drain, and set aside. Remove and discard the large coarse leaves from stems and cut off about ½ inch of the tough lower part of stalks. Wash thoroughly and peel stalks with vegetable peeler. Cut stalks in half lengthwise and then into ½-inch pieces.

2. In a heavy 5-quart pot, heat olive oil over medium-low heat. Add onion and celery and cook, stirring frequently, until vegetables are limp, about 3 minutes. (If vegetables start to stick to bottom of pan, stir in 2 tablespoons broth to prevent scorching.) Add broccoli stems, broth, sage, salt, and pepper flakes. Bring to a boil and add tubettini. Cook, uncovered, over medium-high heat until the pasta is barely al dente, about 7 minutes. Add florets and continue cooking until pasta and florets are cooked, about 5 minutes. Transfer to bowls, sprinkle each with 1 teaspoon Parmesan cheese, and serve.

PER SERVING: Cal. 142   Chol. 2 mg
                     Fat 4 gm   Sod. 228 mg

Cold Curly Endive Soup

[Zuppa di Scarola Riccia]

▦

MAKES 8 CUPS, SERVES 6

A refreshing soup served cold during the summer months and equally good served hot throughout the rest of the year.

2 heads curly endive (about 2 pounds) (see Note)
2 tablespoons olive oil
½ cup thinly sliced scallions
5 cups Chicken Broth, preferably homemade (page 5), or defatted low-sodium canned
1 tablespoon chopped fresh basil leaves or 1 teaspoon crumbled dried basil
2 teaspoons minced fresh thyme or ¾ teaspoon crumbled dried thyme

1 tablespoon minced garlic
¼ cup minced Italian parsley leaves
½ teaspoon coarse salt
½ teaspoon freshly milled black pepper
1½ tablespoons balsamic vinegar
2 small plum tomatoes (4 ounces), blanched, peeled, halved, cored, seeded, and cut into ¼-inch dice, for garnish

1. Discard any wilted or bruised leaves from curly endive. Separate leaves and cut off tough bottom ends of greens (about 3 inches) and discard. Wash greens several times in tepid water to get rid of sand. Thoroughly drain in colander. Slice greens into ½-inch lengths; set aside.
2. In a 5-quart pot, heat oil over low heat. Add scallions and cook, stirring frequently, until soft, about 2 minutes. Add broth and bring to a boil over medium-high heat. Stir in the curly endive, basil, and thyme. Turn heat to low and simmer soup, partially covered, until the curly endive is tender, about 20 minutes. Remove from heat.
3. In a small bowl, combine garlic, 2 tablespoons of the parsley, and salt. Mash with the back of a fork to paste consistency. Stir the garlic paste, remaining 2 tablespoons of parsley, and pepper into

soup. Let soup cool completely to room temperature and stir balsamic vinegar into cooled soup. (Soup can be made up to 4 hours before serving.)

4. Ladle into small bowls, preferably glass, garnish each with diced tomatoes, and serve.

Note: Curly endive, in the same family as escarole, is sometimes called curly chicory. If it is unavailable, you can substitute escarole.

PER SERVING: Cal. 95   Chol. 0 mg
              Fat 5 gm   Sod. 189 mg

Spring Vegetable Soup
[Zuppa Primavera]

◼

MAKES 6 CUPS, SERVES 4

A lighter variation on the more familiar Italian vegetable soups, it makes an excellent first course or complete meal at lunchtime.

1½ tablespoons olive oil
1   cup finely chopped scallions
1   teaspoon minced garlic
2   medium boiling potatoes (8 ounces), peeled, and cut into ¼-inch dice
3½ cups Beef Broth, preferably homemade (page 4), or defatted low-sodium canned
1   pound thin asparagus, washed, trimmed, and cut into 1-inch pieces (see Note)

2   medium zucchini (8 ounces), washed, trimmed, and cut into ½-inch dice
2   teaspoons minced fresh thyme or ½ teaspoon crumbled dried thyme
½   teaspoon coarse salt
½   teaspoon freshly ground black pepper

In a heavy 5-quart saucepan, heat oil over low heat. Add scallions and cook, stirring constantly, until they are soft but not brown, about 2 minutes. Stir in garlic and cook another 30 seconds. Add potatoes and

1 cup of the broth. Cook until potatoes are barely tender, about 4 minutes. Add the remaining broth, 1 cup water, asparagus, and zucchini. Bring to a boil over medium heat. Turn heat to low and cook, partially covered, until vegetables are tender, about 12 to 15 minutes. Stir in thyme and season with salt and pepper. (Soup can be made up to 3 hours before serving. Reheat over low heat.) Ladle into individual bowls and serve.

Note: If thin asparagus spears are unavailable, you can use medium-size ones but they must be peeled with a vegetable peeler from base to spear, leaving tips intact, before cutting into 1-inch pieces.

PER SERVING: Cal. 140   Chol. 0 mg
Fat 6 gm   Sod. 237 mg

Yellow Split-Pea Soup

[Zuppa di Piselli Secco]

MAKES 10 CUPS, SERVES 6

If you prefer a chunky-style soup, do not purée in food processor. Just stir in the mint before serving and garnish with grated carrot.

1½ tablespoons olive oil
1 cup chopped onion
1 pound dried yellow split peas, picked over to remove any foreign matter, rinsed, and drained
2 cups thinly sliced peeled carrots
½ cup thinly sliced peeled parsnips
¾ cup thinly sliced celery, strings removed before slicing

1 bay leaf
2½ quarts Chicken Broth, preferably homemade (page 5), or defatted low-sodium canned
½ teaspoon coarse salt
½ teaspoon freshly milled white pepper
1 tablespoon minced fresh mint or 1 teaspoon crumbled dried mint
¼ cup finely grated carrot, for garnish

1. In a heavy 5-quart pot, heat oil over low heat. Add onion and cook, stirring frequently until soft, about 4 minutes. Add the split peas, carrots, parsnips, celery, bay leaf, and broth. Cover pot and bring to a boil over medium heat. As soon as it reaches a boil, turn heat to low and simmer, partially covered, stirring frequently, until split peas are tender, about 1 hour. Season with salt and pepper, remove from heat, and let soup cool almost to room temperature. Remove bay leaf.
2. Ladle 3 cups of soup at a time into food processor. Run machine nonstop until you have a creamy purée. Transfer soup to a clean pot and repeat until all the soup is puréed. (Soup can be made up to 3 hours before serving. It will definitely thicken as it stands. If desired, it may be thinned with ½ to 1 cup water.)
3. Reheat soup over low heat. Stir in mint, ladle into individual bowls, garnish with grated carrot, and serve.

PER SERVING: Cal. 371   Chol. 0 mg
              Fat 6 gm   Sod. 232 mg

Tuscan Bean Soup with Croutons

[Ribollita]

◼

MAKES 12 CUPS, SERVES 8

There are many variations to this thick, rustic-style bean soup. The following is the version I grew up with.

½ pound dried white kidney or Great Northern beans, picked over to remove any foreign matter

2 tablespoons olive oil

½ cup finely chopped onion

1 teaspoon minced garlic

½ cup finely chopped celery, strings removed before chopping

½ cup finely chopped peeled carrots

5 cups Chicken Broth, preferably homemade (page 5), or defatted low-sodium canned

2 teaspoons minced fresh sage or ¾ teaspoon crumbled dried sage

½ teaspoon coarse salt

½ teaspoon freshly milled black pepper

Eight 1-inch-thick slices day-old Italian bread, crust removed, cut into ½-inch cubes and very lightly toasted

3 tablespoons dry bread crumbs, lightly toasted

3 tablespoons minced Italian parsley leaves

8 teaspoons freshly grated imported Parmesan cheese

1. Place beans in a large bowl, cover with 3 cups cold water, and soak overnight. (Alternatively, you can combine beans and water in a 5-quart pot, bring to a boil, and boil, uncovered, 3 minutes; cover and let stand 1 hour.)

2. Drain beans and place in a 5-quart pot. Add 6 cups cold water, cover pot, and bring to a boil over medium heat. Reduce heat to low and cook until beans are tender, about 1 hour. Drain beans in

strainer and let cool slightly. Place half of the beans in food processor and process until they are puréed. (Or you can pass them through a food mill to purée.) Combine puréed and whole beans; set aside.

3. In a 6-quart pot, heat oil over medium heat. Add onions, garlic, celery, and carrots, and cook, stirring frequently, until soft but not brown, about 5 minutes. Add beans, broth, sage, salt, and pepper. Cover pot and bring to a boil over medium heat. Turn heat to low and simmer, covered, stirring once or twice, for 30 minutes. Stir in toasted bread cubes and cook for another 10 minutes.

4. In a small bowl, combine toasted bread crumbs, parsley, and Parmesan cheese.

5. Ladle soup into individual bowls. Sprinkle about 1 tablespoon bread crumb mixture over each and serve.

PER SERVING: Cal. 248   Chol. 2 mg
              Fat 5 gm   Sod. 352 mg

Winter Vegetable Soup

[Minestrone]

✶

MAKES 12 CUPS, SERVES 8

I just love making this hearty winter minestrone which is chock-full of vegetables. Like most vegetable soups, this is best made at least 4 hours before serving so that all the flavors have a chance to develop and combine. You may even want a second bowl when you check the calorie count on this one.

2   tablespoons olive oil

1   large leek (4 ounces), trimmed, split in half lengthwise, thoroughly washed, and thinly sliced

1   cup diced peeled carrots

½   cup thinly sliced celery, strings removed before slicing

3   medium boiling potatoes (12 ounces), peeled and cut into ¼-inch dice

1   small head savoy cabbage (8 ounces), washed, quartered, cored, and coarsely grated

1   tablespoon minced fresh basil or 1 teaspoon crumbled dried basil

6   cups Vegetable Broth, preferably homemade (page 6), or defatted low-sodium canned chicken broth

2   medium zucchini (8 ounces), washed, trimmed, and cut into ½-inch dice

3   cups well-packed spinach leaves, thoroughly washed and coarsely chopped

One   16-ounce can kidney beans, rinsed and well drained

½   teaspoon coarse salt

½   teaspoon freshly milled black pepper

3   tablespoons minced Italian parsley leaves

1.   In a heavy 6-quart pot, heat oil over low heat. Add leek, carrots, and celery. Cook, stirring frequently, just until vegetables are soft, about 5 minutes. (If vegetables start to stick to bottom of pan, stir in 2 tablespoons broth to prevent scorching.) Add potatoes, cab-

bage, basil, and broth. Cover pot and bring to a boil over medium heat. Cook, stirring frequently, until vegetables are tender, about 30 minutes.

2. Stir in zucchini and cook until barely tender, about 5 minutes. Stir in spinach and kidney beans. Cook until spinach is tender, about 3 minutes. Season with salt and pepper. Remove from heat. (Soup can be made up to 3 hours before serving.)

3. Reheat soup over low heat and stir in parsley. Ladle into individual bowls and serve.

PER SERVING: Cal. 140   Chol. 0 mg
                Fat 4 gm   Sod. 222 mg

Pasta

Introduction

Whenever the word pasta *is mentioned, it brings back memories of my fourth-grade health class. The school nurse asked everyone to name their favorite food. I promptly raised my hand and said, "Pasta." Most of the students sitting around me looked puzzled. "What's that?" one asked. My reply was "Spaghetti," and with that I watched my classmates smile. Several, in fact, later shared with me their affection for spaghetti and meatballs. True, back in those days most Americans only knew pasta as spaghetti and meatballs.*

Today many people think pasta is high in fat and calories. It certainly can be, if one makes a steady diet of lasagne or fettuccine Alfredo. In this chapter, I have re-created the traditional taste of many classic Italian favorites, updating and lightening recipes to fit our contemporary life-style. Even though more than half the fat has been cut from these regional favorites, their old-fashioned flavors have not been sacrificed.

Pasta is one of the most filling complex carbohydrate dishes you can eat. Beside being economical, many recipes are designed for people who have little time to prepare meals. There are several simple sauces that can be cooked while the water is coming to a boil so that dinner can be on the table in less than an hour.

I welcome you to the many family favorites that follow. You will soon realize that pasta is much more than spaghetti and meatballs and much healthier than fettuccine Alfredo. It is, in fact, a primary and popular part of today's luscious and lean Italian cooking.

Light Tomato Sauce

[Salsa di Pomodoro]

3 CUPS

This basic sauce is incorporated into several recipes in this book. In recipes requiring 1½ cups of sauce, I recommend making the full recipe and freezing half. If doubling the recipe, increase cooking time to 40 minutes.

2 tablespoons olive oil
⅓ cup finely minced red onion
⅓ cup finely minced peeled carrots
1½ teaspoons minced garlic
One 28-ounce can Italian plum tomatoes, coarsely chopped, juice included (can be chopped in food processor)

½ teaspoon coarse salt
½ teaspoon freshly milled black pepper
1 teaspoon sugar
2 tablespoons minced fresh basil or 2 teaspoons crumbled dried basil

In a 12-inch skillet, heat oil over medium heat. Turn heat to low; add onion and carrot. Cook, stirring constantly, until soft but not brown, about 4 minutes. Add garlic and continue to cook for an additional minute. Stir in tomatoes, salt, pepper, sugar, and basil. Turn heat to high and bring to a boil. Reduce heat to medium and cook, stirring frequently, until slightly thickened, about 25 minutes. Remove from heat, cover pan, and let sauce rest for at least 1 hour before using.

PER ½ CUP: Cal. 78   Chol. 0 mg
             Fat 4 gm   Sod. 341 mg

~~~~~~

Conchiglie with Scallops

[Conchiglie con Pettine]

◼

SERVES 4

A sweet-tasting sauce with just a tingle of hotness; for scallop lovers it's a definite favorite.

1 pound sea or bay scallops

2 tablespoons plus 2 teaspoons extra virgin olive oil

½ cup fresh bread crumbs made from cubed Italian or French bread, including crust, coarsely ground in food processor or blender

2 tablespoons minced Italian parsley leaves

1 tablespoon minced garlic

6 large ripe plum tomatoes (1 pound), blanched, peeled, cored, seeded, and coarsely chopped

½ teaspoon coarse salt

½ teaspoon crushed red pepper flakes

12 ounces conchiglie (medium-size shell pasta)

1. Wash scallops several times in cold water to remove sand. Blot dry with paper towel. If using bay scallops, leave whole; if using sea scallops, cut horizontally into ½-inch slices; set aside.

2. In a small nonstick skillet, heat 2 teaspoons oil over medium heat. Add bread crumbs and toast until golden, stirring frequently to prevent scorching. Remove from heat and stir in minced parsley.

3. In a 12-inch skillet, heat remaining 2 tablespoons oil over medium heat. Add garlic, turn heat to low, and cook until very lightly golden. Add the tomatoes and simmer, mashing down the tomato pulp with a wooden spoon. Cook until sauce comes to a slow boil, about 1 minute. Stir in scallops and cook, stirring frequently, for 3 minutes. Season with salt and pepper flakes. Remove from heat.

4. Cook pasta in 6 quarts boiling water with 2 teaspoons coarse salt until al dente. Drain pasta and transfer to 4 serving bowls. Spoon sauce over each portion. Sprinkle each serving with toasted bread crumbs and serve.

PER SERVING: Cal. 538   Chol. 37 mg
            Fat 11 gm   Sod. 708 mg

Farfalle with Asparagus and Lemon

[Farfalle con Asparagi]

※

SERVES 4

A good pasta combination for early spring when asparagus are abundant at the market. Try to select asparagus all the same size to ensure even cooking.

1¼ pounds medium-size asparagus	½ teaspoon coarse salt
2 tablespoons olive oil	2 teaspoons freshly milled black pepper
½ cup thinly sliced scallions	2 teaspoons grated lemon peel
2 teaspoons minced garlic	12 ounces farfalle (bows)
½ cup dry vermouth	8 teaspoons freshly grated imported Parmesan cheese, for serving
2 tablespoons strained fresh lemon juice	

1. Wash asparagus several times in cold water to get rid of sand. Using a sharp knife, cut off woody ends at base of spears. With a vegetable peeler, peel stalks from the base of the spear up, leaving tips intact. Slice stalks diagonally into 2-inch lengths; reserve tips.
2. In a deep 12-inch skillet, heat oil over low heat. Add scallions and cook until tender-crisp, about 1 minute. Add garlic and cook for 1 minute. Stir in sliced asparagus stalks and vermouth. Cook, partially covered, until stalks are barely tender when tested with the tip of a knife, about 3 minutes. Add asparagus tips and continue cooking, partially covered, until tender. Stir in lemon juice, season with coarse salt and pepper, and cook for another minute. Stir in lemon rind and remove from heat.
3. While vegetables are simmering, cook pasta in 6 quarts boiling water with 2 teaspoons coarse salt until al dente. Drain pasta in colander; transfer to bowl. Toss with ¾ of the vegetable mixture

and spoon remaining mixture on top. Serve with freshly grated Parmesan cheese.

PER SERVING: Cal. 422   Chol. 3 mg
              Fat 10 gm   Sod. 563 mg

Elbows with Chick-Peas

[Pasta con Ceci]

SERVES 4

This is one pasta dish I make when I am pressed for time and want dinner served in less than one hour. Allowing this dish to rest for 5 minutes before serving enhances the flavor by letting the pasta absorb most of the broth.

2 tablespoons olive oil
1 cup finely chopped celery, strings removed before chopping
½ cup finely minced onion
2 teaspoons minced garlic
One 19-ounce can chick-peas, rinsed and well drained
1½ cups Chicken Broth, preferably homemade (page 5), or defatted low-sodium canned

½ teaspoon coarse salt
½ teaspoon freshly milled black pepper
1 tablespoon minced fresh sage or 1 teaspoon crumbled sage
8 ounces elbow pasta
3 tablespoons minced Italian parsley leaves
8 teaspoons freshly grated imported Parmesan cheese, for serving

1. In a heavy 4-quart saucepan, heat oil over low heat. Add celery and cook, covered, until barely tender, about 2 minutes. Add onion and cook, stirring frequently, until slightly softened, about 2 minutes. Add garlic and continue cooking, stirring frequently, un-

~~~~~~

til slightly softened, about 1 minute. Stir in chick-peas, broth, salt, pepper, and sage. Cook, covered, for an additional 5 minutes.

2. Cook pasta in 6 quarts boiling water with 2 teaspoons coarse salt until barely al dente. Drain pasta and return to pot in which it was boiled. Stir in chick-pea mixture, cover pot, and let rest for 5 minutes before serving. Stir in parsley; ladle into 4 bowls. Serve with freshly grated Parmesan cheese.

PER SERVING: Cal. 406   Chol. 3 mg
               Fat 11 gm   Sod. 648 mg

Fedelini with Roasted Pepper Pesto

[Fedelini con Pesto di Peppe Arrostiti]

SERVES 6

My family always hums happily whenever I prepare this brilliant red pesto sauce. If fedelini is unavailable, you may substitute any thin pasta such as spaghettini or vermicelli.

4   large firm red bell peppers (2 pounds), roasted and peeled (see page 135, for roasting technique)
¼   cup well-packed Italian parsley leaves
½   cup well-packed fresh basil leaves
2   medium cloves garlic, peeled and quartered
2   tablespoons extra virgin olive oil
½   teaspoon coarse salt

½   teaspoon freshly milled black pepper
1½ cups Chicken Broth, preferably homemade (page 5), or defatted low-sodium canned
1   pound fedelini (thin spaghetti)
2   tablespoons snipped fresh basil leaves for garnish
¼   cup freshly grated imported Parmesan cheese, for serving

1. Remove 4 strips of roasted peppers. Slice each into ½-inch lengths and reserve for garnish.

2. In food processor, place remaining roasted peppers, parsley, basil, garlic, extra virgin olive oil, salt, pepper, and 1 cup broth; reserve remaining broth. Process for 20 seconds. Stop machine, and scrape down inside work bowl with plastic spatula. Run machine until you have a smooth purée, about 40 seconds. Transfer pesto to small bowl. Pesto can be made up to 2 hours before cooking pasta. Cover with plastic wrap and leave at room temperature.

3. Cook pasta in 6 quarts boiling water with 2 teaspoons coarse salt until al dente. Drain and transfer to pasta bowl and toss with pesto. Add remaining ½ cup broth and toss once again. Arrange reserved pepper strips in an outside border on top of pasta, garnish with basil, and serve with Parmesan cheese.

PER SERVING: Cal. 387   Chol. 3 mg
                    Fat 7 gm   Sod. 217 mg

~~~~~~

Fusilli with Carrots, Zucchini, and Mint

[Fusilli con Carote e Zucchini]

SERVES 4

A question frequently asked by my students is what type of fusilli to buy for this dish. Fusilli comes in two shapes—quite different but given the same name. The one you want for this dish is the long twisted shape that looks like a corkscrew. If unavailable, purchase linguine or spaghetti; both work equally well.

2 tablespoons olive oil
1½ tablespoons minced garlic
1½ cups coarsely grated peeled carrots
1¼ cups Chicken Broth, preferably homemade (page 5), or defatted low-sodium canned

1½ cups coarsely grated washed and trimmed zucchini
½ teaspoon coarse salt
½ teaspoon freshly milled black pepper
12 ounces long fusilli (twisted like a corkscrew)
¼ cup minced fresh mint leaves

1. In a 12-inch skillet, heat oil over medium heat. Add garlic; turn heat to low and sauté just until soft, but not brown, about 1 minute. Stir in carrots and broth; cook until carrots are barely tender, about 1 minute. Add zucchini and cook, stirring frequently, until barely tender, about 2 minutes. Season with salt and pepper; remove from heat.
2. Cook pasta in 6 quarts boiling water with 2 teaspoons coarse salt until al dente. Drain and transfer to bowl. Toss with vegetable mixture and half of the mint. Sprinkle remaining mint on top and serve.

PER SERVING: Cal. 375   Chol. 0 mg
                Fat 6 gm   Sod. 509 mg

Fusilli with Fava Beans and Peas

[Fusilli con Fava e Piselle]

SERVES 4

The type of fusilli to purchase for this Sicilian classic is the short spiral pasta. Fava beans are usually available at the market from late spring through early summer.

2 pounds medium-size fava beans

1 medium fennel bulb with leaves, about 12 ounces weighed with 2 inches of stalk

2 tablespoons olive oil

1 cup thinly sliced scallions

One 9-ounce package tiny frozen peas, defrosted and well drained

1 cup Chicken Broth, preferably homemade (page 5), or defatted low-sodium canned

½ teaspoon freshly ground black pepper

12 ounces short fusilli spirals

8 teaspoons freshly grated imported Parmesan cheese, for serving

1. Cut off tips of each fava bean pod with a knife. Press along seam to open pod and expose the beans. Lift the green beans out of the cushioned pod. With the tip of a small paring knife, remove small stems that remain attached to beans. Blanch beans in 2 cups boiling water for 30 seconds, drain, and rinse with cold water. With tip of knife slit each skin and pop out bean; set aside.

2. Remove the small feathery leaves from top of fennel stalks, finely chop and reserve ¼ cup for garnish. Cut off and discard stalks. Trim base of bulb. With a vegetable peeler, lightly peel outside of bulb to remove strings. Slice bulb in half vertically and remove center core with a V cut. Thinly slice bulb lengthwise into 1½-inch strips; set aside.

3. In a 3-quart saucepan, heat oil over medium heat. Add fennel slices, turn heat to low, cover pan, and cook until barely ten-

der, about 3 minutes. Add scallions, turn heat to medium, and cook, stirring frequently, until tender-crisp, about 1 minute. Add favas, peas, and chicken broth. Cook, covered, until favas and peas are tender (test by tasting), about 5 minutes. Season with pepper.

4. Cook pasta in 6 quarts boiling water with 2 teaspoons coarse salt until al dente. Drain pasta, transfer to bowl, and toss with bean mixture. Garnish with fennel leaves and serve with Parmesan cheese.

PER SERVING: Cal. 525   Chol. 3 mg
                Fat 10 gm   Sod. 531 mg

Lasagne Pinwheels with Light Tomato Sauce

[Rotolo di Lasagne Riccie con Pomodoro]

SERVES 6

Curly lasagne noodles are available with either one or both sides rippled. Make sure to select the double curly or rippled edge lasagne noodles for this dish. They are often sold with the word Riccie appearing on the label.

Single recipe Light Tomato Sauce (page 19)
1½ cups part-skim ricotta cheese
¼ cup freshly grated imported Parmesan cheese
2 tablespoons minced Italian parsley leaves
1 teaspoon freshly grated lemon rind
¼ teaspoon freshly grated nutmeg
¼ teaspoon coarse salt
½ teaspoon freshly milled black pepper
1 large egg white
12 strips (10 ounces) curly lasagne noodles
12 short sprigs Italian parsley leaves (optional garnish)

1. Prepare sauce 1 hour before cooking lasagne strips.
2. In a medium-size bowl, combine ricotta, 2 tablespoons Parmesan, parsley, lemon rind, nutmeg, salt, and pepper; mix well with fork. Add egg white and blend thoroughly; set aside.
3. Bring 6 quarts of water to a boil and add 2 teaspoons coarse salt. Drop lasagne strips, one at a time, into boiling water. (Dropping one at a time will prevent them from sticking together.) Cook until barely tender, about 4 minutes. Drain in colander and refresh under cold water; drain again.
4. Cover work surface with a large dish towel. Place lasagne strips on work surface with narrow end facing you. Using a narrow metal spatula, evenly spread one heaping tablespoon of filling over each strip. Beginning at narrow end, roll up jelly-roll fashion.
5. Evenly spread ¾ cup of sauce in bottom of a 9 × 13 × 2-inch ovenproof baking dish. Place pasta rolls in baking dish, seam side down and spoon 1 tablespoon sauce over each roll. Place a lightly oiled piece of parchment paper over pasta rolls and cover top of dish with foil. (Lasagne pinwheels can be completely assembled up to 5 hours before baking and refrigerated. Remove from refrigerator ½ hour before baking.)
6. Adjust oven rack to center of oven and preheat to 350°F. Bake pasta rolls in preheated oven for 40 minutes. Remove from oven and let rest for at least 10 minutes before serving.
7. While pasta is resting, reheat remaining sauce. Discard foil and parchment paper. Place two pasta rolls on each plate, spoon 2 tablespoons sauce and 2 teaspoons Parmesan cheese over each serving. Garnish each roll with a parsley sprig and serve.

PER SERVING: Cal. 361   Chol. 22 mg
              Fat 11 gm   Sod. 729 mg

Linguine with Broccoli

[Linguine con Broccoli]

SERVES 4

This recipe is for the harried cook who wants a meal on the table in 30 minutes. Cooking the broccoli and linguine together not only saves you a pot to clean but also makes for a tastier sauce. Make sure you drain the pasta through a colander lined with dampened cheesecloth so you don't lose any tiny pieces of broccoli.

1 large bunch broccoli (about 1½ pounds)	½ teaspoon freshly milled black pepper
12 ounces linguine	8 teaspoons freshly grated imported Parmesan cheese, for serving
2 tablespoons olive oil	
1 tablespoon minced garlic	
½ teaspoon coarse salt	

1. Remove florets from broccoli, leaving about ½ inch of stems. Cut or break into 1-inch pieces. Wash in cold water, drain, and set aside. Remove and discard the large coarse leaves from stems and cut off about ½ inch of the tough lower part of stalk. Wash thoroughly and peel stalks with vegetable peeler. Cut stalks in half lengthwise and into 1-inch pieces.
2. Bring 6 quarts of water to a boil and add 2 teaspoons coarse salt. Add broccoli stalks and cook until barely tender when tested with a fork, about 5 minutes. Add florets and pasta; cook until pasta is al dente.
3. While pasta is cooking, heat oil in a 1-quart saucepan over low heat. Sauté garlic until very lightly golden; remove from heat and stir in ½ cup of the pasta water. Season with salt and pepper.
4. Drain pasta in a colander lined with dampened cheesecloth to prevent tiny pieces of broccoli from falling through holes. Transfer to bowl and toss with sautéed garlic mixture. Serve with freshly grated Parmesan cheese.

PER SERVING: Cal. 437   Chol. 3 mg
                Fat 10 gm   Sod. 594 mg

~~~~~~

Linguine with Fresh Herbs

[Linguine con Erbe Aromatiche]

SERVES 6

I sampled this aromatic pasta dish for the first time in a little trattoria in Pisa. It is now one of my favorites during the summer months when my herb garden is bursting with lush leafy basil, mint, parsley, and thyme.

3 tablespoons plus 1 teaspoon extra virgin olive oil

1 cup fresh bread crumbs made from cubed Italian or French bread, including crust, coarsely ground in food processor or blender

½ cup finely chopped red onion

2 teaspoons minced garlic

¾ cup Chicken Broth, preferably homemade (page 5), or defatted low-sodium canned

½ teaspoon coarse salt

½ teaspoon crushed red pepper flakes

½ cup loosely packed chopped fresh basil leaves

⅓ cup loosely packed chopped fresh mint leaves

½ cup loosely packed chopped Italian parsley leaves

3 tablespoons minced fresh thyme

1 pound linguine

1. In a 10-inch nonstick skillet, heat 1 teaspoon oil over medium heat. Add bread crumbs and toast until golden, stirring frequently to prevent scorching. Remove from heat and transfer to a small bowl.

2. In same skillet, heat remaining 3 tablespoons oil over low heat. Add onion and sauté, stirring frequently, until soft but not brown, about 2 minutes. Add garlic and cook until soft, about 30 seconds. Stir in chicken broth and simmer until heated. Season with salt and red pepper flakes. Transfer mixture to pasta bowl, add fresh herbs, and stir to combine.

3. Cook pasta in 6 quarts boiling water with 2 teaspoons coarse salt until al dente. Drain pasta, transfer to pasta bowl, and toss with herb mixture. Sprinkle toasted bread crumbs on top and serve.

PER SERVING: Cal. 389   Chol. .08 mg
            Fat 9 gm   Sod. 442 mg

Linguine with Sun-Dried Tomato Pesto

[Linguine con Pesto di Pomodoro Secco]

SERVES 6

This do-ahead pesto sauce is a breeze to make with the aid of a food processor and goes extremely well with linguine.

¾ cup sun-dried tomatoes, not packed in oil

¼ cup pitted oil-cured olives or Kalamata olives

½ cup well-packed Italian parsley leaves

½ cup well-packed fresh basil leaves

2 medium shallots (2 ounces), peeled and coarsely chopped

2 tablespoons extra virgin olive oil

½ teaspoon coarse salt

½ teaspoon freshly milled black pepper

1⅓ cups Vegetable Broth, preferably homemade (page 6), or defatted low-sodium canned chicken broth

1 pound linguine

2 tablespoons minced Italian parsley leaves, for garnish

¼ cup freshly grated imported Parmesan cheese, for serving

1. Place sun-dried tomatoes in a bowl and pour on boiling water to cover. Let stand 2 minutes to soften, and thoroughly drain.
2. In food processor, place tomatoes, olives, parsley, basil, shallots, oil, salt, pepper, and 1 cup broth; reserve remaining broth. Process for 20 seconds. Stop machine and scrape down inside of work bowl with plastic spatula. Run machine until tomatoes and olives are finely minced, about 20 seconds. Transfer pesto to small bowl. (Pesto can be made up to 3 hours before cooking pasta. Cover with plastic wrap and leave at room temperature.)
3. Cook pasta in 6 quarts boiling water with 2 teaspoons coarse salt until al dente. Drain and transfer to pasta bowl and toss with ¾ of the pesto. Add remaining ⅓ cup broth and toss once again.

Spoon remaining pesto on top of pasta, garnish with parsley, and serve with Parmesan cheese.

PER SERVING: Cal. 403   Chol. 3 mg
Fat 9 gm   Sod. 676 mg

Pasta Salad with Green Beans, Summer Squash, and Roasted Peppers

[Insalata d'Estate con Penne]

▦

SERVES 6

This fanciful presentation with a rainbow of vegetables is best served at room temperature and no longer than 2 hours after it is made so that the pasta remains moist.

1 pound green beans, washed and trimmed

2 medium-size yellow squash (8 ounces total weight), well scrubbed

12 ounces penne, or any short tubular pasta

2 tablespoons extra virgin olive oil

2 tablespoons balsamic vinegar

1 cup Chicken Broth, preferably homemade (page 5), or defatted low-sodium canned, heated to lukewarm

¾ cup scallions, white part and 2 inches of green, cut into 1-inch lengths

½ cup basil leaves

¼ cup Italian parsley leaves

½ teaspoon coarse salt

½ teaspoon freshly milled black pepper

1 large red bell pepper (8 ounces) roasted (see page 135) and sliced into 1- by ¼-inch strips

¼ cup snipped tops of scallions, for garnish

1. Bring 6 quarts of water to a boil. Add green beans and cook until tender, about 5 minutes. With a slotted spoon, transfer beans to a colander, refresh under cold water, drain well, and blot dry. Slice beans diagonally into 1¼-inch lengths. Transfer to bowl; set aside.

2. In same water, cook squash until barely tender, about 4 minutes. With a slotted spoon, transfer to a colander, refresh under cold water, drain well. Trim ends and slice in half lengthwise. Scoop out seeds with a melon baller and discard. Slice into 1- by ¼-inch strips; combine with green beans.

3. Return water in which beans and squash were cooked to a boil. Add 2 teaspoons coarse salt and cook pasta until al dente. Drain pasta and transfer to bowl.

4. While pasta is cooking, place oil, vinegar, broth, scallions, basil leaves, parsley, salt, and pepper in food processor; process until scallions and herbs are finely minced. Toss dressing with hot pasta, cover with plastic wrap and let cool to room temperature, about 45 minutes. Add green beans and squash and toss. (Pasta salad can be made up to 2 hours before serving. Cover with plastic wrap and leave at room temperature.) When ready to serve, add half of the roasted peppers and toss again. Garnish with remaining peppers and snipped scallion tops.

PER SERVING: Cal. 300   Chol. 0 mg
              Fat 6 gm   Sod. 335 mg

Spaghetti with Uncooked Tomato Sauce

[Spaghetti con Pomodoro Crudo]

SERVES 6

This refreshing sauce should only be made during the summer months when well-ripened plum tomatoes are at their peak.

14 large ripe plum tomatoes (2¼ pounds)	1 teaspoon sugar
2½ tablespoons extra virgin olive oil	¼ cup minced fresh basil
	3 tablespoons minced Italian parsley leaves
3 large cloves garlic, peeled and sliced paper-thin	1 pound spaghetti
½ teaspoon coarse salt	¼ cup freshly grated imported Parmesan cheese, for serving
½ teaspoon freshly milled black pepper	

1. Cut a cross in the bottom end of each tomato (this will make peeling easier after blanching). Plump tomatoes in boiling water for 1 minute. Rinse under cold water and remove skins. Cut each tomato in half lengthwise, remove core, and squeeze each half to remove most of the seeds. Coarsely chop tomatoes and place in strainer over a bowl; reserve juice.

2. Heat oil in 12-inch skillet over medium high heat. Add garlic, turn heat to low, and cook until lightly golden, pressing the garlic flat with a wooden spoon. With a slotted spoon, remove garlic and discard. (If you are a garlic lover, leave it in pan.)

3. Add chopped tomatoes and immediately cover with lid to prevent oil from splashing. Turn heat to low, remove lid, and stir tomatoes just to incorporate with the oil, about 30 seconds. Remove pan from heat, add salt, pepper, sugar, basil, and parsley; mix well.

4. Cook pasta in 6 quarts boiling water with 2 teaspoons coarse salt until al dente. Drain and transfer to bowl and toss pasta with ¾

of the sauce. If pasta is a little dry when tossing, add some of the reserved tomato juice to moisten and toss again. Spoon remaining sauce on top and serve with Parmesan cheese.

PER SERVING: Cal. 390   Chol. 3 mg
                Fat 9 gm   Sod. 476 mg

Spaghetti with Tomato, Arugula, and Olives

[Spaghetti alla Palmina]

SERVES 4

The combination of slightly wilted, bitter arugula and coarsely chopped black olives is beautifully balanced by the bright acid-sweet taste of tomatoes for this savory sauce. This sauce is also delicious served over Polenta (page 41).

2 tablespoons extra virgin olive oil	½ teaspoon coarse salt
2 teaspoons minced garlic	½ teaspoon freshly milled black pepper
6 well-ripened plum tomatoes (1 pound), blanched, peeled, cored, and coarsely chopped	2 tablespoons (about 10) pitted and coarsely chopped oil-cured olives
2½ cups well-packed arugula leaves, thoroughly washed, drained, and coarsely chopped (stems discarded)	12 ounces spaghetti
	8 teaspoons freshly grated imported Parmesan cheese, for serving

1. In a heavy 3½-quart saucepan, heat oil over low heat. Add garlic and sauté until very lightly golden. Add chopped tomatoes and

turn heat to medium. Cook, stirring and mashing a few tomatoes with the back of a wooden spoon, for 2 minutes. Stir in arugula and cook until wilted, about 1 minute. Season with salt and pepper; stir in black olives and cook for another minute.

2.   As sauce is being prepared, cook pasta in 6 quarts boiling water with 2 teaspoons coarse salt until al dente. Drain pasta in colander; transfer to bowl. Toss with ¾ of the vegetable mixture; spoon remaining mixture on top. Serve with freshly grated Parmesan cheese.

PER SERVING: Cal. 437   Chol. 3 mg
                           Fat 11 gm   Sod. 724 mg

Spaghettini with Light Tomato Sauce
[Spaghettini con Salsa di Pomodoro]

SERVES 6

An all-time favorite sauce for any season. I prefer serving it with spaghettini, but it is equally delectable with other thin pastas such as capellini or vermicelli.

Single recipe of Light Tomato
   Sauce (page 19)
3   tablespoons minced Italian
   parsley leaves

1   pound spaghettini
¼   cup freshly grated
   imported Parmesan cheese,
   for serving

1.   Reheat sauce over low heat while cooking pasta. Stir parsley into sauce just before tossing with pasta.
2.   Cook pasta in 6 quarts boiling water with 2 teaspoons coarse salt until al dente. Drain pasta in colander, transfer to bowl, and toss with ¾ of the sauce. Spoon remaining sauce on top and serve with Parmesan cheese.

PER SERVING: Cal. 377   Chol. 3 mg
                           Fat 7 gm   Sod. 681 mg

Vermicelli with Shrimp

[Vermicelli con Gamberi]

▦

SERVES 4

This piquant Ligurian sauce is ready in minutes and guaranteed to please all seafood lovers.

2 tablespoons plus 2 teaspoons olive oil	1 pound large shrimp, shelled, deveined, thoroughly washed, and blotted dry
½ cup minced red onion	
½ cup minced red bell pepper	
½ cup minced celery	½ teaspoon coarse salt
2 teaspoons minced garlic	½ teaspoon freshly milled black pepper
1 cup Chicken Broth, preferably homemade (page 5), or defatted low-sodium canned	2 teaspoons minced fresh thyme or ¾ teaspoon crumbled dried thyme
1½ tablespoons strained lemon juice	12 ounces vermicelli
	2 tablespoons minced Italian parsley leaves, for garnish

1. In a deep 12-inch skillet, heat oil over low heat. Add onion, bell pepper, and celery. Cook, partially covered, until slightly softened, about 3 minutes. (If vegetables start to stick to bottom of pan, stir in a couple of tablespoons of broth to loosen.) Add garlic and cook for another minute. Stir in broth and lemon juice and simmer sauce, stirring frequently, for 10 minutes. Add the shrimp and cook until they turn pink, about 2 to 3 minutes. Season with salt and pepper, stir in thyme, and remove from heat.
2. Cook pasta in 6 quarts boiling water with 2 teaspoons coarse salt until al dente. Drain in colander and transfer to bowl. Push shrimp to one side of pan and toss pasta with vegetable mixture. Spoon shrimp on top of pasta, garnish with minced parsley, and serve.

PER SERVING:　Cal. 518　　Chol. 139 mg
　　　　　　　　Fat 12 gm　Sod. 644 mg

Vermicelli with Ricotta Cream Sauce

[Vermicelli con Salsa di Ricotta]

SERVES 4

This is the fastest pasta sauce in this chapter to prepare. Vermicelli pasta paired with this creamy sauce and topped with parsley is a very filling one-course meal. I usually serve the Bibb, Watercress, Cucumber, and Radish Salad (page 148) to round it off.

1½ cup part-skim ricotta cheese, room temperature

½ cup skim milk, room temperature

2 tablespoons freshly grated imported Parmesan cheese

1 teaspoon grated lemon rind

¼ teaspoon freshly grated nutmeg

2 tablespoons snipped chives, or top green part of scallion

¼ cup well-packed Italian parsley leaves

¼ teaspoon coarse salt

½ teaspoon freshly grated white pepper

12 ounces vermicelli

2 teaspoons minced Italian parsley leaves, for garnish

1. In food processor, place ricotta cheese, milk, Parmesan cheese, lemon rind, nutmeg, snipped chives, parsley, salt, and pepper. Process until chives are finely minced and ricotta has the texture of lightly whipped cream, about 45 seconds.
2. Cook pasta in 6 quarts boiling water with 2 teaspoons coarse salt until al dente. Drain pasta and return to pot in which it was boiled. Quickly toss pasta with the cream sauce. Transfer to 4 pasta bowls. Garnish each with ½ teaspoon parsley and serve.

PER SERVING: Cal. 350   Chol. 24 mg
              Fat 8 gm   Sod. 454 mg

Polenta and Rice

Introduction

While many Italians eat pasta several times a week, polenta and rice perform the same function in the meal. They may be served either as an accompaniment to meat, fish, and poultry or as a main course.

Polenta (cooked yellow cornmeal) is a hearty dish that, in my mother's household, was usually served during the winter months. Today, I serve it as an alternative to pasta. It can be topped off with a mushroom sauce or any of the vegetable sauces found in the pasta chapter of this book. Grilled herbed polenta is a simple but wonderful accompaniment to any grilled entrée.

Two types of cornmeal are used in making polenta: coarse-grained cornmeal, available in Italian specialty shops and health food stores, and fine-grained cornmeal such as Quaker's, available in supermarkets. The coarse-grained variety requires stirring the mixture constantly over heat for at least 45 minutes. For recipes in this chapter, I recommend using Quaker's fine-grained cornmeal, which cooks in approximately 12 minutes and will produce absolutely perfect polenta. Also helpful for today's busy cook is an excellent instant variety available in Italian specialty stores.

Rice is another versatile food in an Italian household. As risotto, it, too, can take the place of pasta, served as a side dish or a main course. In this chapter, I offer two vibrant vegetable risottos, one with zucchini and red bell peppers and another with asparagus, carrot, and scallions topped off with ricotta cheese. To make risotto, Arborio rice, a short-grain variety grown in northern Italy, is used. When properly cooked, this rice is both moist and tender, with grains that have a tendency to cling together and provide a nuttier flavor than the common long-grain variety. Arborio rice is available in Italian specialty stores and many supermarkets today.

For the other rice recipes found in this book, you may use Arborio or any long-grained white variety.

Basic Recipe for Polenta

YIELDS ABOUT 3 CUPS
COOKED POLENTA

1 cup Quaker yellow cornmeal
1¼ cups water

2 cups Chicken Broth,
preferably homemade (page
5), or defatted low-sodium
canned
¼ teaspoon coarse salt

1. In a medium bowl, mix cornmeal and water with a fork until you have a smooth paste.
2. In a heavy 3½-quart saucepan, bring broth to a boil and add salt. Add the cornmeal paste, stirring constantly with a wooden spoon. Bring mixture to a boil, then turn heat to low. Cook the polenta, stirring frequently to keep the mixture smooth. If some lumps form in cooking, push them against the sides of the pan with spoon to dissolve. Polenta will be done when mixture is very thick and starts to come away from the sides of pan, about 10 to 12 minutes.
3. The following recipes give suggestions for serving.

PER CUP: Cal. 200   Chol. 0 mg
          Fat 1 gm   Sod. 150 mg

Creamy Polenta with Kale and Kidney Beans

[Polenta alla Stabiano]

SERVES 6

During the winter months, thoughts turn to comfort foods like this sturdy and flavorful creamy polenta dish. This has become a favorite of mine and of many of my students.

Single recipe Braised Kale and Kidney Beans (page 133)
1 Basic Recipe for Polenta (page 41)
½ to 1 cup heated Chicken Broth, preferably homemade (page 5), or defatted low-sodium canned
¼ cup freshly grated imported Parmesan cheese, for serving

1. Prepare the braised kale and beans up to 3 hours before cooking polenta. Reheat over low heat while cooking polenta.
2. As soon as polenta is cooked, slowly stir in ½ cup of heated broth and whisk the polenta until very creamy. At this point the polenta should fall from a spoon in a continuous stream. If still too thick, stir in remaining broth, a little at a time, until creamy.
3. Ladle the polenta into 6 soup plates. Spoon kale and beans over polenta. Sprinkle 2 teaspoons Parmesan cheese over each dish and serve.

PER SERVING: Cal. 268   Chol. 3 mg
Fat 8 gm   Sod. 470 mg

Polenta with Mushroom Sauce

[Polenta con Salsa di Funghi]

SERVES 4

This hearty Tuscan dish with sautéed mushrooms, aromatic wine, broth, and herbs was once considered peasant fare. Not so any longer; soothing, delicious food like this is now appreciated for its simple goodness.

2 tablespoons extra virgin olive oil
2 teaspoons minced garlic
½ pound crimini mushrooms, trimmed, wiped, and thinly sliced
1 cup Beef Broth, preferably homemade (page 4), or ½ cup defatted low-sodium canned broth diluted with ½ cup water

2 tablespoons dry red wine
1 tablespoon minced fresh rosemary or 1 teaspoon crumbled dried rosemary
½ teaspoon coarse salt
½ teaspoon freshly milled black pepper
1 Basic Recipe for Polenta (page 41)
2 tablespoons minced Italian parsley leaves

1. In a 10-inch skillet, heat oil over medium heat. Add garlic, turn heat to low, and cook until soft but not brown. Add mushrooms and sauté, stirring frequently, until tender, about 3 minutes. Add broth and wine and simmer until liquid is reduced by half, about 10 to 15 minutes. Stir in rosemary, salt, and pepper. Cover pan and remove from heat.
2. Make polenta. As soon as polenta is cooked, transfer to a platter and spread evenly with metal spatula.
3. Reheat mushroom sauce over low heat and spoon over polenta. Sprinkle with parsley and serve.

PER SERVING: Cal. 239   Chol. 0 mg
              Fat 9 gm   Sod. 312 mg

Baked Polenta with Light Tomato Sauce

[Polenta al Forno]

⬛

SERVES 4

This layered polenta dish can be completely assembled one day ahead of serving, covered with plastic wrap and refrigerated overnight. Remove plastic wrap and bring back to room temperature 2 hours before baking.

1½ cups Light Tomato Sauce
     (page 19)
  1 Basic Recipe for Polenta
     (page 41)

2 tablespoons grated
   Parmesan cheese

1. Make the light tomato sauce up to 4 hours before cooking polenta.
2. Adjust rack to center of oven and preheat to 375°F.
3. Spread ½ cup tomato sauce in a shallow round 2-quart ovenproof casserole. Spoon polenta on top and spread evenly with a narrow metal spatula. Spread remaining sauce on top evenly with spatula. Sprinkle with grated cheese.
4. Bake until cheese is thoroughly melted and top forms a light crust, about 25 to 30 minutes. Remove from oven and let rest for at least 10 minutes before serving.
5. To serve, slice into wedges and lift out with metal spatula.

PER SERVING: Cal. 222   Chol. 2 mg
               Fat 6 gm   Sod. 425 mg

Grilled Polenta with Sage

[Polenta Arrostito]

▨

SERVES 4

Basil, mint, or thyme may be substituted for the sage. Polenta can also be broiled in the oven 4 inches from heat source on a broiler pan lightly sprayed with vegetable cooking spray. An excellent side dish with any of the grilled meat or poultry dishes in this book.

1 Basic Recipe for Polenta (page 41)	1 tablespoon minced fresh sage or 1 teaspoon crumbled dried sage
¼ teaspoon coarse salt	
½ teaspoon freshly milled black pepper	

1. As soon as polenta is cooked, remove from heat and stir in salt, pepper, and sage.
2. Spray an 8 × 8 × 2-inch metal baking pan with cooking spray. Spoon polenta into pan and smooth surface with a metal spatula. Cover with plastic wrap and cool to room temperature. Refrigerate until firm and well chilled, about 3 hours or overnight.
3. Lightly grease grill rack with cooking spray. Preheat charcoal grill until coals have turned a gray ashy color. Preheat gas grill according to manufacturer's suggested time on high heat.
4. Run a knife around inside edge of pan to loosen polenta. Invert onto a board and cut into 4 even pieces. Place polenta on grill and cook, turning once, until golden brown and laced with grill marks on both sides, about 4 to 5 minutes per side. Transfer to platter and serve.

PER SERVING: Cal. 150   Chol. 0 mg
            Fat 1 gm   Sod. 203 mg

Rice with Lemon

[Riso con Limone]

SERVES 4

This lemony rice is a good accompaniment to any of the grilled or broiled lamb dishes in this book.

2 tablespoons olive oil
½ cup thinly sliced scallions
1 cup Arborio or long-grain rice, picked over to remove any dark grains
2¼ cups water
3 tablespoons strained lemon juice

½ teaspoon coarse salt
½ teaspoon freshly milled white pepper
1 tablespoon grated lemon rind
2 tablespoons minced Italian parsley leaves

In a heavy 5-quart saucepan, heat oil over medium heat. Add scallions, turn heat to low, and cook, stirring constantly, until slightly softened, about 2 minutes. Add rice and stir constantly until opaque and well coated with oil. Add water and lemon juice and turn heat to high. As soon as liquid comes to a boil, cover pan, turn heat to low, and simmer until rice is tender and all the liquid is absorbed, about 20 minutes. Season with salt and pepper. Remove from heat and let rice rest covered for 10 minutes before serving. Stir in lemon rind and parsley, transfer to bowl, and serve.

PER SERVING: Cal. 237   Chol. 0 mg
              Fat 7 gm   Sod. 190 mg

Rice with Tomato and Yellow Squash

[Riso alla Zia Lucia]

SERVES 4

When finished, this rice dish becomes pale red and exudes the vibrant flavor of tomatoes with just a tinge of hotness. An excellent side dish with Veal Scallops and Marsala Wine Sauce (page 66).

2 tablespoons olive oil

½ cup minced red onion

3 well-ripened plum tomatoes (8 ounces), blanched, peeled, halved, cored, seeded, and coarsely chopped

2 small yellow squash (8 ounces), washed, trimmed, quartered lengthwise, and cut crosswise into ½-inch slices

1 cup Arborio or long-grain rice, picked over to remove any dark grains

3 cups Vegetable Broth, preferably homemade (page 6) or defatted low-sodium canned chicken broth

1 tablespoon minced fresh thyme or 1 teaspoon crumbled dried thyme

½ teaspoon coarse salt

¼ teaspoon crushed red pepper flakes

2 tablespoons minced Italian parsley leaves

In a heavy 5-quart saucepan, heat oil over medium heat. Add onion and cook until soft but not brown, about 3 minutes. Add tomatoes and cook, stirring constantly, for 1 minute. Stir in squash and rice. Add broth and turn heat to high. As soon as broth comes to a boil, cover pan, turn heat to low, and simmer until rice is tender and all the liquid is absorbed, about 20 minutes. Stir in thyme and season with salt and pepper flakes. Remove from heat and let rice rest, covered, for 10 minutes before serving. Stir in parsley, transfer to bowl, and serve.

PER SERVING: Cal. 275   Chol. 0 mg
              Fat 8 gm   Sod. 208 mg

Rice with Spinach

[Riso con Spinaci]

SERVES 4

This speckled green and white rice dish is an excellent plate mate with a piece of Roasted Chicken with Vinegar and Rosemary (page 96).

1 cup long-grain white rice, picked over to remove any dark grains
2 tablespoons olive oil
1 teaspoon minced garlic
2 cups well-packed spinach leaves, thoroughly washed, drained, and coarsely chopped

½ teaspoon freshly grated nutmeg
½ teaspoon coarse salt
½ teaspoon freshly milled black pepper

1. In a 5-quart pot, bring 3 quarts water to a rolling boil over high heat. Add rice and stir once with a wooden spoon so the rice does not stick to the bottom of pot. When water returns to a boil, reduce the heat and simmer, uncovered, until tender, about 12 to 15 minutes. Drain in a fine mesh strainer.

2. While rice is cooking, heat oil in a 12-inch skillet over medium heat. Add garlic, turn heat to low, and cook, stirring constantly, until lightly golden, about 1 minute. Add spinach, cover pan, and cook until spinach is wilted, about 2 minutes. Season with nutmeg, salt, and pepper. Stir cooked rice into skillet and stir to combine. Remove from heat, transfer to bowl, and serve.

PER SERVING: Cal. 240   Chol. 0 mg
                Fat 7 gm   Sod. 213 mg

Rice with Peas and Mint

[Riso con Piselli e Menta]

SERVES 4

No one in our family cooked rice in as many different ways as my mother. One that was always a favorite was this dish of rice with peas. Almost as creamy as a risotto, but much easier to make.

2 tablespoons olive oil
½ cup finely chopped onion
1 cup Arborio or long-grain rice, picked over to remove any dark grains
3 cups Chicken Broth, preferably homemade (page 5), or 2 cups defatted low-sodium canned broth diluted with 1 cup water

One 9-ounce package tiny frozen peas, defrosted and well drained
½ teaspoon coarse salt
½ teaspoon freshly milled white pepper
3 tablespoons minced fresh mint or 1½ teaspoons crumbled dried mint

1. In a heavy 5-quart saucepan, heat oil over medium heat. Add onion and cook until soft but not brown, about 3 minutes. Add rice and stir constantly until opaque and well coated with oil. Add broth and turn heat to high. As soon as broth comes to a boil, cover pan, turn heat to low, and simmer for 20 minutes.
2. Stir peas into rice mixture. Cover pan and continue to simmer over low heat for another 2 minutes. Season with salt and pepper. Remove pan from heat and let rice rest, covered, for 10 minutes before serving. Stir in mint, transfer to bowl, and serve.

PER SERVING: Cal. 299   Chol. 0 mg
            Fat 8 gm   Sod. 303 mg

Rice Salad

[Insalata di Riso]

▦

SERVES 6

This is a taste-enlivening dish to serve during the summer season with something simple, like Amy's Grilled Chicken Breasts (page 89).

3　tablespoons extra virgin olive oil

1　small eggplant (1 pound), trimmed, peeled, and cut into ½-inch dice

1¼　cups Arborio or long-grain rice, picked over to remove any dark grains

1　medium yellow bell pepper (5 ounces), halved, cored, seeded, and cut into ½-inch dice

2　medium well-ripened tomatoes (8 ounces), halved, cored, and finely chopped

¼　cup minced red onion

1　teaspoon minced garlic

2　tablespoons minced Italian parsley leaves

1　tablespoon minced fresh mint or 1 teaspoon crumbled dried mint

1　teaspoon minced fresh oregano or ¼ teaspoon crumbled dried oregano

2　tablespoons strained lemon juice

½　teaspoon coarse salt

½　teaspoon freshly milled black pepper

1. In a 10-inch nonstick skillet, heat 1 tablespoon oil over medium heat. Add eggplant, turn heat to low, and cook, partially covered, stirring frequently, until tender, about 7 minutes. Remove from heat and let cool to room temperature.

2. In a 6-quart pot, bring 4 quarts water to a rolling boil over high heat. Add rice and stir once with a wooden spoon so the rice does not stick to the bottom of pot. When water returns to a boil, reduce the heat to low and simmer, uncovered, until tender, about 12 to 15 minutes. Drain in strainer and refresh under cold water. Drain again and transfer to bowl.

3. Add cooled eggplant, bell pepper, tomatoes, onion, garlic, parsley, mint, and oregano. Toss well to combine.

4. In a small bowl, whisk together the lemon juice, salt, and pepper. Add remaining 2 tablespoons oil and whisk until well combined. Pour dressing over salad and gently mix with 2 forks. (Salad can be prepared up to 2 hours before serving. Cover with plastic wrap and leave at room temperature. Toss once again before serving.)

PER SERVING: Cal. 234   Chol. 0 mg
              Fat 7 gm   Sod. 132 mg

Risotto with Asparagus

[Risotto con Asparagi]

SERVES 4

Lightness is the essential character of this risotto. When finished, the asparagus will still be tender-crisp. Topped off with a dollop of ricotta and the piquant herbal accent of minced parsley and chives, this makes for a great main course entrée.

1½ pounds medium-size asparagus
4 to 4½ cups Vegetable Broth, preferably homemade (page 6), or defatted low-sodium canned chicken broth
1½ tablespoons olive oil
1 cup thinly sliced scallions
½ cup finely chopped peeled carrot
¼ cup finely chopped celery, strings removed before chopping

1¼ cups Arborio rice, picked over to remove any dark grains
½ teaspoon coarse salt
½ teaspoon freshly milled black pepper
¼ cup part-skim ricotta cheese
2 tablespoons minced Italian parsley leaves
1 tablespoon minced chives or green part of scallion

1. Wash asparagus several times in cold water to get rid of sand. Using a sharp knife, cut off woody ends at base of spear. With a vegetable peeler, peel stalks from the base of the spear up, leaving tips intact. Slice stalks diagonally into 2-inch lengths; reserve tips.

2. In a 5-quart saucepan, bring broth to a boil over medium heat. Add sliced asparagus stalks and cook until barely tender, about 3 minutes. Add asparagus tips and continue cooking until tender-crisp, about 1 minute. Using a slotted spoon, transfer asparagus to a bowl. Keep the broth at a bare simmer over low heat.

3. In a heavy 5-quart saucepan, heat oil over medium heat. Add scallions, carrot, and celery, turn heat to low, and cook, stirring frequently with wooden spoon until soft, about 3 minutes. (If vegetables start to stick to bottom of pan, add ¼ cup broth to prevent scorching.) Add rice and stir until grains turn opaque. Add 1 cup simmering broth to the rice and cook over low heat, stirring constantly, until all the liquid has been absorbed. Watch carefully so the rice does not stick to bottom of pan. Add more broth, 1 cup at a time, stirring constantly, and cooking the mixture until liquid is absorbed after each addition. When rice has finished cooking, the risotto should have a creamy consistency. Test by tasting a few grains; it should be soft on the outside and just a little bit chewy on the inside. Total cooking time will be approximately 25 to 30 minutes. Stir in asparagus and cook another 30 seconds. Season with salt and pepper and remove from heat. Transfer to individual bowls. Top each serving with 1 tablespoon ricotta. Sprinkle with parsley and chives and serve.

PER SERVING: Cal. 339   Chol. 5 mg
               Fat 7 gm   Sod. 245 mg

~~~~~~

Risotto with Zucchini and Red Peppers

[Risotto con Zucchini e Pepe Rosso]

▓

SERVES 6

This risotto always reminds me of the Italian flag with its broad stripes of red, white, and green. When properly cooked, the zucchini and peppers will retain their crunchy texture.

5½ to 6 cups Chicken Broth, preferably homemade (page 5), or defatted low-sodium canned broth

4 small zucchini (1 pound), washed, trimmed, and cut into strips 1 inch long by ½ inch wide

2 medium red bell peppers (12 ounces), halved, cored, seeded, and cut into strips 1 inch long by ½ inch wide

2 tablespoons olive oil

1 medium leek, trimmed to white part and 3 inches of the green, halved, thoroughly washed, and finely chopped to make 1½ cups

2 cups Arborio rice, picked over to remove any dark grains

½ cup dry white wine

½ teaspoon coarse salt

½ teaspoon freshly milled black pepper

3 tablespoons minced Italian parsley leaves

¼ cup freshly grated Parmesan cheese, for serving

1. In a 6-quart saucepan, bring broth to a boil over medium heat. Add the zucchini and pepper strips. Turn heat to low and simmer until vegetables are barely tender, about 3 minutes. Using a slotted spoon, transfer vegetables to a bowl. Keep the broth at a bare simmer over low heat.

2. In a heavy 5-quart saucepan, heat oil over medium heat. Add leek,

turn heat to low, and cook, stirring frequently with wooden spoon, until soft, about 3 minutes. Add the rice and stir until opaque and well coated with oil. Add the wine and cook mixture, stirring constantly, until all the liquid has been absorbed, about 1½ minutes. Add 1½ cups broth to the rice and cook over low heat, stirring constantly, until all the liquid has been absorbed. Watch carefully so the rice does not stick to bottom of pan. Add more broth, 1 cup at a time, stirring constantly and cooking the mixture until all the liquid is absorbed after each addition. After 4½ cups of broth have been added, the rice should be barely tender. Stir in the zucchini, pepper strips, and another 1 cup of the broth. Simmer the mixture, stirring constantly for an additional 3 to 4 minutes or until the liquid is absorbed. The rice should be soft on the outside and a bit chewy on the inside. If necessary, add an additional ½ cup broth and cook the mixture in the same manner until the rice is tender. Total cooking time will be approximately 30 to 35 minutes. Remove pan from heat, season with salt and pepper. Stir in minced parsley. Transfer to individual bowls, and sprinkle 2 teaspoons Parmesan cheese on each serving.

PER SERVING: Cal. 348   Chol. 3 mg
              Fat 7 gm   Sod. 250 mg

Meats

Introduction

Beef

GRILLED MARINATED FLANK STEAK

HAMBURGERS PARMIGIANA

PEPPERED FILET MIGNON WITH CRIMINI MUSHROOMS

STUFFED STEAK ROLLS

TUSCAN BEEF STEW

Veal

HERB- AND LEMON-COATED VEAL CUTLETS

VEAL CHOPS WITH ROSEMARY AND ORANGE SAUCE

VEAL SCALLOPS WITH MARSALA WINE SAUCE

VEAL SCALLOPS WITH TOMATO AND SAGE

VEAL STEW

Lamb

CRUSTY BROILED LAMB CHOPS WITH WINE SAUCE

LAMB STEW NEAPOLITAN STYLE

PIQUANT GRILLED LAMB STEAKS

LAMB CHOPS WITH SCALLION-MINT SAUCE

ROAST LEG OF LAMB WITH HERBS

Pork

BRAISED PORK CHOPS

GRILLED PORK CHOPS WITH SAGE

CRUSTY OVEN-BAKED PORK CHOPS

PORK ROAST AMADEO

PORK TENDERLOINS WITH ORANGE AND FENNEL

PORK MEDALLIONS WITH ROASTED PEPPERS AND ROSEMARY

STUFFED PORK CHOPS

While a decade ago many Americans focused on meat as the mainstay of their daily diet, today's life-style changes have altered that situation drastically. We are finding our plates filled with more complex carbohydrates and smaller portions of meat. In essence, this "new" style mirrors the traditional Italian diet, where a small piece of meat was served in conjunction with several vegetables or preceded by a moderate portion of pasta, polenta, risotto, or soup.

As you read through this chapter, note that the recipes recommend the choicest, leanest cuts of meat available, such as flank steak, pork tenderloin, veal scallops, and leg of lamb. If you have trouble finding a good selection, either go to a private butcher or ask the butcher in your supermarket to assist you in choosing, cutting, and trimming meats.

The recipes in this chapter are prepared in a variety of healthy styles: broiling, braising, sautéing, and grilling. They represent different regions of Italy and capture authentic tastes with a maximum of flavor and a minimum of fat.

Grilled Marinated Flank Steak

[Bistecca Gustoso]

SERVES 6

For best flavor, make sure to marinate the steak at least 4 hours. Actual cooking time will be under 10 minutes. Serve this medium-rare, as well-done flank steak is not tender.

2 teaspoons minced garlic

1 tablespoon grated rind of navel orange

½ cup strained fresh orange juice

2 tablespoons white wine vinegar

¼ teaspoon cayenne pepper

1 teaspoon Dijon-style mustard

1 tablespoon minced fresh mint or 1 teaspoon crumbled dried mint

One 1½-pound flank steak, well trimmed of fat

2 large navel oranges, peeled, halved, and thinly sliced

8 short sprigs fresh mint, for garnish

1. In a shallow glass or ceramic dish, combine garlic, orange rind, juice, vinegar, pepper, mustard, and mint. Add steak to marinade; turn once to coat. Cover with plastic wrap and refrigerate for at least 4 hours, turning steak twice in marinade. Remove steak from marinade, scraping any bits of marinade clinging to meat back into bowl. Transfer marinade to small saucepan and bring to a boil; reserve.

2. Lightly grease grill rack with vegetable cooking spray. Preheat charcoal grill until coals have turned a gray ashy color, or preheat gas grill according to manufacturer's suggested time on high heat.

3. Place steak on grill 4 inches from heat source and sear 1½ minutes on each side. Brush with a little reserved marinade and continue cooking, covered (with lid down or tented with foil), for approximately 4 minutes, brushing frequently with marinade. (Make a little slit in center of steak to check for doneness. Steak should be

pink inside.) Transfer to carving board, tent with foil, and let rest for 7 minutes before slicing.

4. Arrange orange slices in overlapping pattern around outside of platter. Slice steak diagonally across the grain into very thin slices. Arrange down center of platter and garnish with mint.

PER SERVING: Cal. 168   Chol. 41 mg
                 Fat 6 gm   Sod. 77 mg

Hamburgers Parmigiana

[Polpetti Parmigiana]

SERVES 6

When cooked, these meat patties remain crisp on the outside while still moist on the inside—a favorite with my grandchildren, John Paul, Colin, Sarah, and Denton.

¼ cup minced scallions
1 tablespoon minced fresh basil leaves or 1 teaspoon crumbled dried basil
1 tablespoon minced Italian parsley leaves
1½ tablespoons freshly grated imported Parmesan cheese
¼ teaspoon freshly grated nutmeg
½ teaspoon freshly milled black pepper

1 cup fine dry bread crumbs
2 large egg whites
1½ pounds very lean ground round or sirloin steak
1 tablespoon water
¾ cup Light Tomato Sauce (page 19)
6 thin slices (3 ounces) part-skim mozzarella cheese

1. Adjust oven rack to upper portion of oven and preheat to 425°F. Lightly grease a shallow baking pan with vegetable cooking spray; set aside.

2. In a deep bowl, combine scallions, basil, parsley, Parmesan cheese, nutmeg, pepper, and ½ cup bread crumbs. Stir in 1 egg white. Add meat and mix well. Shape into 6 oval patties.

3. In a small bowl, beat remaining egg white with water. Place remaining ½ cup bread crumbs on a piece of wax paper. Dip patties in egg white mixture and thoroughly coat with bread crumbs. Place in prepared pan and bake until coating is crisp and lightly golden, about 15 minutes. Remove from oven and spoon 2 tablespoons tomato sauce over each patty. Place one slice of cheese on top of each and return to oven. Bake until sauce begins to bubble and cheese is melted, about 5 minutes. Transfer to platter and serve.

PER SERVING: Cal. 351   Chol. 81 mg
                Fat 18 gm   Sod. 380 mg

Peppered Filet Mignon with Crimini Mushrooms

[Bistecca all'Anna]

SERVES 4

Coated with coarsely ground pepper, cooked medium-rare, and topped off with a mushroom wine sauce, these steaks make a beautiful presentation for special guests.

Four 5-ounce filet mignon steaks, each 1 inch thick, well trimmed of fat	6 ounces crimini or button mushrooms, wiped, stems discarded, and sliced ¼ inch thick
4 teaspoons coarsely ground black pepper	⅓ cup dry red wine
2 tablespoons olive oil	½ teaspoon coarse salt
¼ cup minced shallots	1 tablespoon minced fresh thyme or 1 teaspoon crumbled dried thyme

1. Place steaks on a flat plate and sprinkle each with ½ teaspoon pepper. Firmly press pepper onto surface of each steak. Turn steaks over and repeat on other side.
2. In a 10-inch skillet, heat 1 tablespoon oil over medium-high heat. Sauté steaks, turning once, until brown and cooked to desired doneness, about 4 minutes per side for medium-rare. Transfer steaks to platter.
3. In same skillet, heat remaining tablespoon of oil over medium-high heat. Add shallots and sauté, scraping any fragments in bottom of pan, for 30 seconds.
4. Add mushrooms and cook until tender, stirring frequently, about 3 minutes. (If mushrooms start to stick to skillet, stir in 2 tablespoons wine.) Add wine to skillet, turn heat to low and simmer for 1 minute. Return steaks and any accumulated juices to skillet. Season with salt, add thyme, and cook steaks just until heated through, about 1 minute. Place steaks on individual plates, spoon mushrooms and pan juices over each, and serve.

PER SERVING: Cal. 322   Chol. 89 mg

Fat 18 gm   Sod. 255 mg

~~~~~~

Stuffed Steak Rolls

[Farsumagru]

SERVES 4

*For a beautiful presentation, arrange beef rolls in center of platter, spoon
a little sauce over each, and serve with a border of Rice with Peas and
Mint (page 49).*

One 1¼-pound slice top round
steak about ½ inch thick,
well trimmed of fat

1 cup Beef Broth, preferably
homemade (page 4), or
defatted low-sodium
canned

¼ pound crimini or button
mushrooms, wiped and
finely minced

1 tablespoon minced Italian
parsley leaves

1½ tablespoons freshly grated
imported Parmesan cheese

½ teaspoon freshly milled
black pepper

½ cup well-packed fresh
bread crumbs from
cubed Italian or French
bread, including crust,
coarsely ground in food
processor or blender

1 large egg white, lightly
beaten

1½ tablespoons olive oil

2 teaspoons minced garlic

1 cup canned Italian plum
tomatoes, coarsely
chopped, juice included

1. Slice steak in half crosswise. Place each slice within a folded piece
    of plastic wrap and pound with a mallet or the broad side of a
    chef's knife to a thickness slightly less than ¼ inch.

2. In a 10-inch nonstick skillet, heat ½ cup beef broth over high heat.
    Add mushrooms and cook, stirring frequently, until no liquid is
    left in bottom of pan. Remove from heat and stir in parsley,
    cheese, pepper, and bread crumbs. Let cool slightly and stir in egg
    white. Spread filling evenly over slices. Roll up jelly-roll style,
    starting from short end. Tie each roll with kitchen twine.

3. Adjust oven rack to center of oven and preheat to 350°F.

4. Wipe out the skillet with paper towels and heat oil over medium-
    high heat. Sear beef rolls on all sides. Transfer rolls to shallow

1-quart ovenproof casserole. Add garlic to skillet and sauté until very lightly golden, scraping up any fragments that might have stuck to bottom of pan. Stir in remaining ½ cup beef broth and the tomatoes. Turn heat to high and cook sauce for 2 minutes. Pour sauce over beef rolls. Cover casserole and bake in preheated oven, basting frequently with sauce, until meat is tender when pierced with tip of knife, about 45 minutes. Transfer rolls to plate, cover with foil, and let rest for 10 minutes before slicing.

5. Remove twine and slice rolls at a slight angle into 1-inch slices. Arrange on platter and spoon a little sauce over each. Serve remaining sauce separately.

PER SERVING: Cal. 258   Chol. 67 mg
              Fat 10 gm   Sod. 282 mg

Tuscan Beef Stew

[Spezzatino di Manzo]

SERVES 4

During the winter season, I serve this hearty, aromatic stew over individual portions of polenta. Try it; you might like it!!

2 tablespoons olive oil
1¼ pounds top round steak, well trimmed of fat and cut into 2-inch cubes
1 cup thinly sliced celery, strings removed before slicing
½ cup chopped peeled carrots
1 cup chopped red onion
¾ cup dry white wine
¼ cup strained lemon juice

1½ cups Beef Broth, preferably homemade (page 4), or defatted low-sodium canned
2 tablespoons minced fresh basil or 2 teaspoons crumbled dried basil
½ teaspoon coarse salt
½ teaspoon freshly milled black pepper
2 tablespoons minced Italian parsley leaves, for garnish

1. In a heavy 4-quart dutch oven, heat oil over medium heat. Add beef and sauté, turning cubes, until lightly browned on all sides. With slotted spoon, transfer cubes to plate. Add celery, carrots, and onion. Cook until barely softened, scraping any fragments that might be stuck to bottom of pan, about 1 minute. If vegetables start to stick to pan, add 2 tablespoons broth.

2. Return beef to pan and add wine. Turn heat to high and cook, stirring frequently, until wine is reduced to 2 tablespoons, about 4 minutes. Stir in lemon juice, broth, basil, salt, and pepper. Turn heat to low and cook, covered, stirring frequently, until meat is extremely tender when pierced with tip of a knife, about 1½ hours. As soon as meat is cooked, uncover pan, turn heat to medium-high, and cook, stirring frequently, until sauce is slightly thickened, about 10 minutes. Transfer to shallow bowl, garnish with parsley, and serve. (Stew can be made up to 3 hours before serving and reheated, covered, over low heat.)

PER SERVING: Cal. 247   Chol. 65 mg
               Fat 11 gm   Sod. 302 mg

Herb- and Lemon-Coated Veal Cutlets

[Cotolette di Vitello con Erbe e Limone]

SERVES 4

The herbs and lemon rind add a flavor bonus to the crusty coating after the cutlets are cooked.

3	tablespoons Gold Medal Wondra flour	1½	tablespoons finely grated lemon rind
2	large egg whites	½	teaspoon coarse salt
1½	tablespoons water	½	teaspoon freshly milled black pepper
1	cup dry bread crumbs	Four	4-ounce veal cutlets, each ¼ inch thick
2	tablespoons minced fresh thyme or 2 teaspoons crumbled dried thyme		
¼	cup minced Italian parsley leaves	2	tablespoons olive oil
		4	lemon wedges, for garnish

1. Place flour on a piece of wax paper. In a shallow bowl, beat egg white and water with a fork. On a flat plate, combine bread crumbs, thyme, parsley, lemon rind, salt, and pepper. Dredge cutlets in flour, dip in beaten egg white mixture and thoroughly coat with bread crumb mixture. Refrigerate cutlets in a single layer on platter lined with wax paper for at least 1 hour to firm up and set coating.

2. In a 12-inch nonstick skillet, heat oil over medium heat. Sauté the cutlets until lightly golden, about 2 minutes on each side. Transfer to platter and garnish with lemon wedges.

PER SERVING: Cal. 288   Chol. 89 mg
              Fat 10 gm   Sod. 378 mg

Veal Chops with Rosemary and Orange Sauce
[Vitello alla Appolloni]

SERVES 4

For years this delicious recipe has held an important place in my collection of old reliables. The recipe was given to me by one of my favorite butchers, my friend Bob Appolloni.

3 tablespoons Gold Medal Wondra flour

½ teaspoon freshly milled black pepper

Four 8-ounce rib veal chops, ½ inch thick, well trimmed of fat

2 tablespoons olive oil

1 cup Chicken Broth, preferably homemade (page 5), or defatted low-sodium canned

½ cup strained fresh orange juice

1 tablespoon minced fresh rosemary or 1 teaspoon crumbled dried rosemary

½ teaspoon coarse salt

1 tablespoon grated rind of navel orange

2 tablespoons minced Italian parsley leaves

1 large navel orange, sliced into ¼-inch rounds (trim off and discard the ends), for garnish

4 sprigs fresh rosemary, for garnish

1. On a piece of wax paper, combine flour and black pepper. Dredge chops in seasoned flour and shake off excess. (Dredge just before cooking or flour coating will become gummy.)
2. In a 12-inch skillet, heat oil over medium-high heat. Sear the chops, turning once, until lightly golden, about 1½ minutes on each side. Add broth, orange juice, and rosemary to skillet. Cook, partially covered, basting frequently, until chops are tender, about 10 minutes. Transfer chops to serving platter and cover loosely with foil.

3. Return pan to high heat and bring broth mixture to a boil. Boil until sauce is reduced to about ⅓ cup, about 3 minutes. Strain sauce through a fine mesh strainer set over a small saucepan. Heat sauce over low heat, adding salt, orange rind, and parsley. Pour any accumulated juices from serving plate into sauce and stir to combine.

4. Spoon sauce over chops. Garnish platter with orange slices and sprigs of fresh rosemary.

PER SERVING: Cal. 299   Chol. 121 mg
               Fat 13 gm   Sod. 333 mg

Veal Scallops with Marsala Wine Sauce

[Scaloppine con Marsala]

SERVES 6

Lightly browned and finished off with dry marsala wine, this veal will be fork tender and delicious enough to be served to any connoisseur of fine food!

3 tablespoons Gold Medal Wondra flour	½ cup dry marsala wine
1 teaspoon freshly milled black pepper	⅓ cup Chicken Broth, preferably homemade (page 5), or defatted low-sodium canned
Twelve 2-ounce veal scallops, each ¼ inch thick	½ teaspoon coarse salt
2 tablespoons olive oil	3 tablespoons minced Italian parsley leaves, for garnish
½ cup minced shallots	

1. On a piece of wax paper, combine flour and pepper. Dredge scallops in seasoned flour. (Dredge just before cooking or flour coating will become gummy.)

2. In a 12-inch nonstick skillet, heat oil over medium-high heat. Sauté veal in two batches until lightly golden, about 1½ minutes per side. Transfer scallops to platter.

3. Turn heat to medium. Add shallots to skillet and cook until lightly golden, scraping up any browned fragments left in bottom of pan. (If shallots start to stick to pan, add 2 tablespoons chicken broth.) Add wine, turn heat to high, and cook, stirring constantly until slightly reduced, about 1 minute. Stir in broth and continue cooking, stirring constantly, until sauce is slightly thickened. Return veal and any juices accumulated on platter to pan, and turn scallops to coat with sauce. Season with salt and cook until veal is heated, about 30 seconds. Transfer to platter and spoon sauce over top. Garnish with parsley and serve.

PER SERVING: Cal. 198   Chol. 74 mg
                Fat 6 gm   Sod. 189 mg

Veal Scallops with Tomato and Sage

[Scaloppine alla Toscana]

SERVES 4

Here's a quick and delicious version of a Tuscan-style scaloppine alive with the flavoring of tomato and sage. I was introduced to this dish while visiting cousins in the quaint city of Lucca.

2 tablespoons olive oil	2 tablespoons minced fresh
Eight 2-ounce veal scallops, each ¼ inch thick	sage leaves or 2 teaspoons crumbled dried sage
½ cup minced red onion	½ teaspoon coarse salt
3 well-ripened plum tomatoes (8 ounces), blanched, peeled, cored, and coarsely chopped	½ teaspoon freshly milled black pepper
	4 clusters of fresh sage leaves, for garnish

1. In a 12-inch skillet, heat oil over medium heat. Sauté veal, turning once, until very lightly golden, about 1½ minutes per side. Transfer veal to platter.
2. Add onion to skillet, turn heat to low, and cook, stirring constantly, until lightly golden, about 2 minutes. Stir in tomatoes and sage. Turn heat to high and cook, stirring frequently, until there is very little liquid left in bottom of pan, about 2 minutes. Return veal to pan, spoon sauce over meat and season with salt and pepper. Cook for an additional minute. Transfer veal to platter, spoon sauce over top, and garnish with sage leaves.

PER SERVING: Cal. 202   Chol. 89 mg
                Fat 9 gm   Sod. 263 mg

Veal Stew

[Spezzatino di Vitello]

▦

SERVES 4

Enriched with the aromatic flavoring of thyme, this traditional-style Ligurian stew makes for a hearty feast. Broccoli with Roasted Peppers and Pine Nuts (page 125) are all this combination needs to make the meal complete.

1½ tablespoons olive oil

1½ pounds boned shoulder of veal, well trimmed of fat and any connecting membranes, cut into 1½-inch cubes

1 large onion (10 ounces), peeled, halved, and thinly sliced

½ teaspoon coarse salt

½ teaspoon freshly milled black pepper

1 tablespoon minced fresh thyme or 1 teaspoon crumbled dried thyme

2 bay leaves

1⅓ cups Chicken Broth, preferably homemade (page 5), or defatted low-sodium canned

3 large carrots (10 ounces), trimmed, peeled, and sliced diagonally into ½-inch pieces

2 large all-purpose potatoes (10 ounces), peeled and cut into 1½-inch cubes

2 tablespoons minced Italian parsley leaves

1. In a 4-quart dutch oven, heat oil over medium heat. Add veal and sauté, stirring frequently, until lightly golden. Using a slotted spoon, transfer veal to a plate. Add onion to dutch oven and sauté, stirring constantly, scraping any fragments that cling to pan, until lightly golden, about 3 minutes. (If onion starts to stick to bottom of pan, add 2 tablespoons broth.)

2. Return veal to pan. Add salt, pepper, thyme, bay leaves, and ¾ cup chicken broth. Turn heat to low and cook, covered, until veal is barely tender when pierced with the tip of a knife, about 30 minutes. Add carrots and cook covered for 5 minutes. Stir in potatoes and remaining broth. Cook, covered, until potatoes are tender, about 12 minutes. Remove bay leaves, stir in parsley, transfer to platter, and serve.

PER SERVING: Cal. 312   Chol. 122 mg
              Fat 10 gm   Sod. 355 mg

~~~~~~

Crusty Broiled Lamb Chops with Wine Sauce

[Agnello con Salsa di Vino]

SERVES 4

A light coating of lemon and bread crumbs seals in juices as the chops broil. Spooning a little wine sauce over each before serving adds a succulent finishing touch.

⅔ cup dry white wine (preferably Orvieto Secco)

1 cup Beef Broth, preferably homemade (page 4), or defatted low-sodium canned

1 tablespoon minced fresh thyme or 1 teaspoon crumbled dried thyme

3 tablespoons minced shallots

3 tablespoons strained fresh lemon juice

¾ cup fine dry bread crumbs

½ teaspoon freshly milled black pepper

Eight 4-ounce rib lamb chops, each about 1 inch thick, well trimmed of fat

1. Remove broiler rack and pan from oven; preheat oven on broil setting for 15 minutes. Lightly grease broiler rack with vegetable cooking spray; set aside.

2. In a small saucepan, combine wine, broth, thyme, and shallots. Bring to a boil over high heat and cook until mixture is reduced to about ⅓ cup, about 7 minutes. (Sauce can be made up to 1 hour before cooking meat. Reheat over low heat while chops are broiling.)

3. Place lemon juice in a small bowl. On a piece of wax paper, combine bread crumbs and pepper. Lightly brush both sides of chops with lemon juice and coat with seasoned bread crumbs. Transfer to broiler rack.

4. Broil chops 4 inches from heat source until surface is slightly crusty, about 3 minutes. Turn chops and continue broiling on second side 2 minutes for medium rare, 3 minutes for medium.
5. Transfer chops to platter, spoon sauce over them, and serve.

PER SERVING: Cal. 270   Chol. 66 mg
               Fat 10 gm   Sod. 252 mg

Lamb Stew Neapolitan Style

[Umido d'Agnello alla Napoletana]

SERVES 6

This Neapolitan-style stew is perfect for a blustery day. The meat is lightly browned and then simmered in a fragrant broth generously flavored with tomato sauce before the vegetables are added.

2 tablespoons olive oil
2 pounds boneless lamb shoulder, well trimmed of fat, cut into 1½-inch pieces
1 large red onion (12 ounces), peeled, halved, and thinly sliced
3 tablespoons tomato paste
1¾ cups Vegetable Broth, preferably homemade (page 6), or defatted low-sodium canned chicken broth
1 tablespoon minced fresh basil or 1 teaspoon crumbled dried basil

2 bay leaves
½ teaspoon coarse salt
¼ teaspoon crushed red pepper flakes
3 large carrots (10 ounces), trimmed, peeled, and sliced diagonally into ½-inch pieces
½ pound green beans, washed, trimmed, and sliced into 1-inch lengths
4 large all-purpose potatoes (1 pound), peeled and cut into 1½-inch cubes

1. In a 5-quart dutch oven, heat oil over medium heat. Add lamb and sauté, stirring frequently, until lightly golden. Using a slotted spoon, transfer lamb to plate. Add onion to dutch oven and sauté until lightly golden, stirring constantly, scraping any fragments that cling to bottom of pan. (If onion starts to stick to bottom of pan, add 2 tablespoons broth.)

2. Dissolve tomato paste in broth and stir into pan. Add basil, bay leaves, salt, and crushed pepper flakes. Return meat to pan. Turn heat to low and cook, covered, until lamb is barely tender when pierced with the tip of a knife, about 1 hour. Add carrots and green beans; cook, covered, until vegetables are barely tender, about 15 minutes. Stir in potatoes and cook until tender, about 12 minutes. Remove bay leaves, transfer to platter, and serve. (Stew can be made up to 2 hours before serving. Reheat over low heat.)

PER SERVING: Cal. 314   Chol. 75 mg
                    Fat 13 gm   Sod. 298 mg

Piquant Grilled Lamb Steaks

[Costoletta d'Agnello Piccante]

SERVES 4

This piquant marinade adds a special zippy flavoring to the steaks when grilled. Stewed Potatoes and Zucchini in Tomato Sauce (page 137) makes an ideal accompaniment.

¼ cup balsamic vinegar
2 teaspoons minced garlic
1½ tablespoons minced fresh rosemary or 1½ teaspoons crumbled dried rosemary
½ teaspoon freshly milled black pepper

Four 6-ounce lamb steaks, cut from leg, well trimmed of fat
4 sprigs fresh rosemary, for garnish

1. In a small bowl, combine vinegar, garlic, rosemary, and black pepper.
2. Place steaks on a platter. Using your fingertips, rub vinegar mixture on both sides of steaks. Marinate at room temperature for 1 hour.
3. Lightly grease grill rack with cooking spray. Preheat charcoal grill until coals have turned a gray ashy color or preheat gas grill according to manufacturer's suggested time on high heat.
4. Remove steaks from marinade and gently blot dry; discard marinade. Place steaks on grill about 4 inches from heat source. Sear meat about 1 minute on each side. Cook steaks an additional 2 minutes on each side for rare, 3 minutes on each side for medium.
5. Transfer steaks to platter, garnish with rosemary sprigs, and serve.

PER SERVING: Cal. 161   Chol. 69 mg
Fat 7 gm   Sod. 54 mg

Lamb Chops
with Scallion - Mint Sauce

[Agnello con Salsa di Menta]

▦

SERVES 6

The sweet and sour sauce is a delightful foil for broiled lamb chops. Serve with Roasted New Potatoes (page 136).

1½ tablespoons olive oil
¾ cup minced scallions
1 cup Chicken Broth, preferably homemade (page 5), or defatted low-sodium canned
2 well-ripened plum tomatoes (4 ounces), blanched, peeled, and finely chopped
2 tablespoons white wine vinegar
2 teaspoons sugar

1½ tablespoons minced fresh mint or 1½ teaspoons crumbled dried mint
½ teaspoon coarse salt
½ teaspoon freshly milled black pepper
Six 6-ounce center-cut loin lamb chops, well trimmed of fat
2 large cloves garlic, split in half
6 short sprigs fresh mint, for garnish

1. In a small nonstick skillet, heat oil over low heat. Add scallions and cook, stirring frequently, until softened, about 3 minutes. Add broth and tomatoes, turn heat to high, and cook until slightly thickened, about 5 minutes. Stir in vinegar, sugar, and mint and cook for another 30 seconds. Season with salt and pepper; remove from heat. (Sauce can be made up to 3 hours before broiling chops. Reheat over low heat while meat is cooking.)

2. Remove broiler rack and pan from oven; preheat oven on broil setting for 15 minutes. Lightly grease broiler rack with vegetable cooking spray; set aside.

3. Place chops on flat plate and rub both sides with garlic. Transfer to rack and broil 4 inches from heat source 3 minutes on each side for medium-rare, 4 minutes on each side for medium.

4. Transfer chops to platter and spoon sauce over top. Garnish with mint sprigs and serve.

PER SERVING: Cal. 191   Chol. 61 mg
              Fat 10 gm   Sod. 187 mg

Roast Leg of Lamb with Herbs

[Arrosto d'Agnello]

SERVES 6

This is the most traditional way to cook roasted leg of lamb throughout central and southern Italy.

One 4-pound leg of lamb cut from shank half, well trimmed of fat

1½ tablespoons minced garlic

1½ tablespoons minced fresh thyme or 1½ teaspoons crumbled dried thyme

1½ tablespoons minced fresh mint or 1½ teaspoons crumbled dried mint

1 tablespoon finely grated lemon rind

⅓ cup strained fresh lemon juice

2 cups Chicken Broth, preferably homemade (page 5), or defatted low-sodium canned

½ teaspoon coarse salt

½ teaspoon freshly milled black pepper

1 large lemon, sliced into 6 wedges, for garnish

6 fresh thyme sprigs, for garnish

1. Adjust oven rack to center of oven and preheat to 400°F.
2. With tip of knife, make slits all around roast approximately 2 inches apart and about 1 inch deep.
3. In a small bowl, combine garlic, thyme, mint, and lemon rind.

Add 2½ tablespoons lemon juice to mixture and combine to form a thin paste. Work paste into the slits, using a demitasse spoon and your fingers. Spread any remaining paste over surface of lamb. Place lamb on a rack in a shallow roasting pan and roast for 20 minutes. Lower oven temperature to 350°F. Pour remaining lemon juice and 1 cup broth over roast. Continue roasting, basting every 15 minutes with pan juices, until thermometer inserted in thickest part of meat registers 135°F. for rare, about 90 minutes. (For medium, the thermometer should register between 145 and 150 degrees F., about 2 hours.) Transfer roast to platter, cover with foil, and let rest 10 minutes before carving.

4. If there are any traces of fat left in roasting pan, remove with a metal spoon. Add ¼ cup water and remaining 1 cup broth to pan and place over medium heat. Scrape up any browned fragments that might be stuck to bottom of pan and cook for 3 minutes. Strain pan juices through a small strainer into a small saucepan. Season with salt and pepper. Keep warm over low heat while carving meat.

5. Carve meat and arrange slices in a slightly overlapping pattern. Garnish with lemon wedges and thyme sprigs. Spoon some pan juices on top of lamb. Serve the remaining juices separately.

PER SERVING   Cal. 304   Chol. 137 mg
                       Fat 11 gm   Sod. 238 mg

Braised Pork Chops

[Maiale alla Louisa]

SERVES 4

Spooning aromatic vegetables over the pork while they cook keeps the chops extremely moist.

3 tablespoons Gold Medal Wondra flour

½ teaspoon freshly milled black pepper

Four 5-ounce center-cut boneless pork chops, each about ½ inch thick, well trimmed of fat

1 tablespoon olive oil

¼ cup dry vermouth

½ cup thinly sliced celery, strings removed before slicing

½ cup thinly sliced onion

1 large yellow pepper (8 ounces), halved, cored, and sliced lengthwise into ¼-inch strips

½ teaspoon coarse salt

1 tablespoon minced rosemary or 1 teaspoon crumbled dried rosemary

1. On a piece of wax paper, combine flour and pepper. Lightly dredge each chop in seasoned flour. (Dredge just before cooking or flour coating will become gummy.)

2. In a 12-inch skillet, heat oil over medium heat. Add chops and sauté until lightly golden, about 3 minutes on each side; transfer chops to plate.

3. Add vermouth to skillet, turn heat to low, and scrape up any fragments left in bottom of pan with wooden spoon. Add celery and cook, stirring frequently, until tender-crisp, about 1 minute. Add onion and pepper strips and cook until slightly softened, about 2 minutes. Season with salt and add rosemary.

4. Return pork to pan and spoon vegetable mixture over chops. Cover pan and cook until pork is tender when tested with the tip of a knife, about 12 to 15 minutes. (If pork starts to stick to bottom of pan, add 2 tablespoons of water.) Transfer chops to platter, spoon vegetable mixture and pan juices on top, and serve.

PER SERVING: Cal. 249   Chol. 72 mg
                Fat 9 gm   Sod. 274 mg

Grilled Pork Chops with Sage

[Costoletta di Maiale al Toscana]

SERVES 4

Make sure to firmly press the sage leaves onto each chop. While grilling, the herb chars a little and adds a delicate flavoring to the meat.

Four 8-ounce center-cut loin
 pork chops, each 1 inch
 thick, well trimmed of fat
 4 teaspoons olive oil
16 fresh large sage leaves

¼ teaspoon coarse salt
¼ teaspoon freshly ground
 black pepper
 4 short sprigs fresh sage, for
 garnish

1. Place chops on a flat plate. With your fingers, rub ½ teaspoon oil on each surface of each chop. (This will prevent sticking when chops are placed on heated grill.) Press 2 sage leaves on each surface of each chop. Let chops stand at room temperature for 1 hour to allow the sage flavor to penetrate the meat.

2. Preheat charcoal grill until coals have turned a gray ashy color. Preheat gas or electric grill according to manufacturer's suggested time.

3. Place chops on grill 4 inches from heat source. Sear the chops for 1 minute on each side, turning meat with long-handled tongs. Cook chops for an additional 4 minutes on each side. To test for doneness, insert the tip of a small knife into the thickest part near the bone. When done, the juices should run clear, with no traces of pink.

4. Transfer to platter, season with salt and pepper, garnish with fresh sage sprigs, and serve immediately.

PER SERVING: Cal. 354   Chol. 107 mg
             Fat 21 gm   Sod. 166 mg

Crusty Oven-Baked Pork Chops

[Coste di Maiale al Forno]

▒

SERVES 4

The crusty coating of Parmesan cheese, thyme, and bread crumbs seals the chops so they are juicy and tender when served.

1½ tablespoons Dijon-style mustard

3 tablespoons water

2 tablespoons finely grated imported Parmesan cheese

1 tablespoon minced fresh thyme or 1 teaspoon crumbled dried thyme

¼ teaspoon coarse salt

½ teaspoon freshly ground black pepper

1½ cups dry bread crumbs

Four 8-ounce center-cut loin pork chops, each 1 inch thick, well trimmed of fat

2 tablespoons olive oil

4 sprigs fresh thyme, for garnish

1. In a shallow bowl, whisk together mustard and water. On a piece of wax paper, combine Parmesan cheese, thyme, salt, pepper, and bread crumbs. Hold one end of each pork chop with your fingertips and lightly brush both surfaces with mustard mixture. Firmly dredge each chop in bread crumb mixture to coat both sides. Refrigerate chops in a single layer on platter lined with wax paper for at least 1 hour (chilling prevents coating from coming off during cooking).

2. Adjust rack to upper portion of oven and preheat to 375°F. Line a shallow baking pan with parchment paper and lightly brush 1 tablespoon oil over surface of paper.

3. Place chops in prepared pan 2 inches apart. Lightly drizzle remaining 1 tablespoon oil over chops and bake in preheated oven until underside is lightly golden and slightly crispy, about 10 minutes (check by lifting with a broad metal spatula). Remove from oven and carefully turn chops with metal spatula. Return to oven and

continue cooking until second side is slightly crispy, about 15 minutes. Transfer to platter, garnish with thyme, and serve.

PER SERVING: Cal. 397   Chol. 99 mg
              Fat 20 gm   Sod. 554 mg

Pork Roast Amadeo

[Maiale alla Papa]

SERVES 6

This was my father's favorite way of preparing a pork roast. Coating the meat with the flour mixture produces a good crusty surface on the roast. Basting with broth and vermouth keeps it juicy and yields a very flavorful gravy.

2 tablespoons Gold Medal Wondra flour
½ teaspoon freshly milled black pepper
1 teaspoon anise seed
One 2-pound boneless pork rib roast, well trimmed of fat
3 whole bay leaves

2 cups Chicken Broth, preferably homemade (page 5), or defatted low-sodium canned
¼ cup dry vermouth
1½ tablespoons arrowroot or cornstarch
¼ teaspoon coarse salt
10 sprigs curly parsley, for garnish

1. Adjust oven rack to center of oven and preheat to 400°F.
2. On a flat plate combine flour, pepper, and anise seed. Dredge roast on all sides in seasoned flour.
3. Place roast on a rack in roasting pan, and arrange bay leaves on top of roast. Place meat in preheated oven and roast for 30 minutes. Reduce oven temperature to 375°F. and pour 1 cup broth

and the vermouth over roast. Continue roasting, basting with pan juices every 15 minutes, for 1 hour. Transfer roast to platter, discard bay leaves, cover loosely with foil and let stand for 15 minutes before slicing.

4. Using a metal spoon, skim off any surface fat from roasting pan. Add ¼ cup water to pan and place over medium heat. Scrape bottom of pan with wooden spoon to loosen any fragments that might be stuck. Strain pan juices through a small strainer into a small saucepan. Dissolve arrowroot in remaining broth and stir into pan juices. Season with salt and cook over medium heat until gravy is slightly thickened, about 1 minute.

5. Carve roast into ½-inch slices. Arrange slices on a platter in a slightly overlapping pattern. Garnish with parsley sprigs. Serve gravy separately.

PER SERVING: Cal. 222   Chol. 64 mg
               Fat 9 gm   Sod. 124 mg

Pork Tenderloins with Orange and Fennel

[Maiale alla Genovese]

SERVES 6

After marinating, the tenderloins are quickly roasted in the oven, sliced, and topped with a fennel-flavored orange sauce.

2 tablespoons finely grated rind of navel orange
1 cup strained fresh orange juice
1 teaspoon minced garlic
1 teaspoon crushed fennel seed
1 tablespoon coarsely chopped sage leaves or 1 teaspoon crumbled sage leaves

2 well-trimmed pork tenderloins (1¾ pounds total weight)
¼ teaspoon coarse salt
¼ teaspoon freshly milled black pepper
6 sprigs fresh sage, for garnish
1 small navel orange, ends trimmed and sliced into thin rounds, for garnish

1. In a 9 × 13 × 2-inch casserole, combine orange rind, juice, garlic, fennel seed, and sage. Place pork tenderloins in casserole and turn to coat completely with marinade. Cover with plastic wrap and marinate at room temperature for 1 hour.
2. Adjust oven rack to center of oven and preheat to 500°F.
3. Remove tenderloins from marinade and place on a rack in a roasting pan; reserve marinade.
4. Place pan in oven and reduce temperature to 475°F. Roast pork until thermometer inserted in center registers 150°F., about 20 to 25 minutes. Transfer tenderloins to platter, cover loosely with foil, and let stand for 10 minutes before slicing.
5. Strain marinade into a small saucepan. Bring to a boil over medium heat and cook until sauce is reduced by half, about 7 minutes. Season with salt and pepper.

~~~~~~

6. Slice tenderloins diagonally into ½-inch slices. Arrange on platter in a slightly overlapping pattern and spoon sauce over meat. Garnish with sage leaves and orange slices.

PER SERVING: Cal. 181   Chol. 86 mg
             Fat 3 gm   Sod. 126 mg

Pork Medallions with Roasted Peppers and Rosemary

[Medaglione di Maiale]

SERVES 4

The roasted peppers and rosemary enhance the flavorful essence of these tender medallions.

One 1¼-pound pork tenderloin, well trimmed
2 tablespoons Gold Medal Wondra flour
½ teaspoon freshly milled black pepper
2 tablespoons olive oil
½ cup finely chopped shallots
½ cup Chicken Broth, preferably homemade (page 5), or defatted low-sodium canned

2 large red bell peppers (1 pound), roasted, peeled, and sliced into ½-inch strips (see page 135 for roasting technique)
1 tablespoon minced fresh rosemary or 1 teaspoon crumbled dried rosemary
½ teaspoon coarse salt
4 sprigs fresh rosemary, for garnish

1. Slice pork tenderloin crosswise into rounds 1 inch thick. Place medallions within a folded piece of plastic wrap and flatten with the broad side of a knife to a thickness of about ½ inch.
2. On a piece of wax paper, combine flour and pepper. Dredge medallions in seasoned flour and shake off excess (dredge just before cooking or flour coating will become gummy).
3. In a 12-inch skillet, heat oil over medium heat. Sauté medallions until lightly golden, about 1 minute on each side; transfer to platter.
4. Add shallots to skillet and sauté, stirring constantly and scraping any fragments that might be stuck to bottom of pan, about 30 seconds. Add broth to pan and bring to a boil. Return pork to skillet and spoon shallot mixture over medallions. Turn heat to low and simmer for 3 minutes. Stir in roasted peppers and rosemary; cook an additional minute. Season with salt and pepper; remove from heat.
5. Transfer medallions to platter and spoon roasted pepper mixture over top. Garnish with rosemary sprigs.

PER SERVING: Cal. 227   Chol. 92 mg
              Fat 11 gm   Sod. 262 mg

~~~~~~

Stuffed Pork Chops

[Involtini di Maiale]

SERVES 4

Simple to prepare and exotic enough to excite anyone who loves stuffed pork chops. This recipe is a favorite of my husband, John.

Four 8-ounce rib pork chops, each 1 inch thick, well trimmed of fat
⅓ cup finely chopped onion
⅓ cup finely chopped celery, strings removed before chopping
⅔ cup Chicken Broth, preferably homemade (page 5), or defatted low-sodium canned
¼ cup seedless dark raisins, plumped in hot water, thoroughly drained, and finely chopped

½ cup well-packed fresh bread crumbs made from cubed Italian or French bread, including crust, coarsely ground in food processor or blender
2 teaspoons minced fresh rosemary or ½ teaspoon crumbled dried rosemary
½ teaspoon coarse salt
½ teaspoon freshly milled black pepper
1½ tablespoons olive oil
4 short sprigs fresh rosemary, for garnish

1. To make a pocket for stuffing, use a sharp knife to cut a horizontal slit down the center and the full length of each chop right to the bone. Place chops on a flat surface and open the pockets.

2. In a small saucepan, cook onion and celery in ⅓ cup broth over low heat, covered, until celery is tender, about 5 minutes.

3. In a medium-size bowl, combine onion, celery, raisins, bread crumbs, rosemary, salt, and pepper. Fill the chops with the stuffing. Bring flaps together to enclose stuffing and fasten each with 2 toothpicks.

4. In a 12-inch skillet, heat oil over medium heat. Add chops and lightly brown on both sides. Remove chops to flat plate. Add remaining broth and scrape any fragments left in bottom of pan with wooden spoon. Return chops to pan. Cover pan and cook over

medium-low heat, basting every 10 minutes with pan juices, until chops are tender when pierced with the tip of the knife, about 20 minutes.

5. Transfer chops to platter, remove toothpicks, pour pan juices over each, garnish with sprigs of rosemary, and serve.

PER SERVING: Cal. 344   Chol. 71 mg
              Fat 15 gm   Sod. 368 mg

Poultry

Introduction

Chicken

AMY'S GRILLED CHICKEN BREASTS

BAKED DRUMSTICKS WITH POTATOES

BRAISED CHICKEN THIGHS WITH TOMATO AND OLIVES

CHICKEN PICCATA

CHICKEN BREASTS WITH MUSHROOMS AND SUN-DRIED TOMATOES

ROASTED CHICKEN WITH VINEGAR AND ROSEMARY

WARM CHICKEN SALAD WITH BALSAMIC DRESSING

Turkey

ROAST TURKEY BREAST WITH LEMON SAUCE

GRILLED TURKEY TENDERLOINS WITH PIMIENTO SAUCE

PEPPERS STUFFED WITH GROUND TURKEY

TURKEY CUTLETS WITH MARSALA WINE SAUCE

Who doesn't love poultry? It's versatile, economical, and considered by many to be the healthiest kind of meat. It's low in calories and saturated fats and very high in protein. No matter how they are prepared—broiled, baked, roasted, grilled, or sautéed—the poultry dishes in this chapter should please all weight-conscious, health-minded people.

To keep fat, cholesterol, and calories to a minimum, it is important to trim off all excess fat. While most recipes call for boneless, skinless poultry, there are a few that call for roasting with the skin on. Make sure to remove the skin before eating. Also note that ground turkey or ground chicken are excellent substitutes in any recipes calling for ground meat.

The poultry selections that follow use oil and salt in moderation, but there is no loss of flavor. Zesty herbs and seasonings, full-bodied wines, and a variety of fragrant wine-based vinegars create delicious dishes that adhere to recommended guidelines for good nutrition.

Amy's Grilled Chicken Breasts

[Petti di Pollo alla Amadea]

SERVES 6

This perfectly seasoned marinade keeps the boneless chicken breast moist while grilling.

Six 5-ounce boneless, skinless chicken breast halves, well trimmed of fat
1 tablespoon Dijon-style mustard
⅓ cup white wine vinegar
1 tablespoon minced garlic
1 tablespoon honey

2 tablespoons minced fresh thyme or 2 teaspoons crumbled dried thyme
½ teaspoon coarse salt
¼ teaspoon crushed red pepper flakes
1½ tablespoons olive oil
6 sprigs fresh thyme, for garnish

1. Place chicken breasts within a folded piece of plastic wrap; slightly flatten upper portion of each breast with the broad side of a chef's knife to promote even grilling. Place breasts in a shallow glass or ceramic dish.
2. Place mustard, vinegar, garlic, honey, thyme, salt, and pepper flakes in a small bowl; stir with fork to combine. Add oil a little at a time and whisk to combine marinade. Pour marinade over breasts. Cover with plastic wrap and marinate in refrigerator, turning once or twice in marinade, for at least 2 hours, or up to 4 hours. Remove breasts from marinade, scraping any bits clinging to chicken back into the shallow dish. Transfer all marinade to small saucepan and bring to a boil; reserve.
3. Lightly grease grill rack with cooking spray. Preheat charcoal grill until coals have turned a gray ashy color, or preheat gas grill according to manufacturer's suggested time on medium heat.
4. Place breasts on grill. Cook covered with lid or tented with foil,

basting frequently with marinade, until tender, approximately 5 to 6 minutes on each side.

5. Transfer to platter, garnish with fresh thyme, and serve.

PER SERVING: Cal. 206   Chol. 82 mg
              Fat 5 gm   Sod. 289 mg

Baked Drumsticks with Potatoes

[Gambe di Pollo alla Pizzaiola]

SERVES 4

A great one-dish meal for those busy days when you don't feel like fussing in the kitchen.

8   large chicken legs (2 pounds 4 ounces total weight)
2   large Idaho or russet potatoes (1¼ pounds), peeled, halved lengthwise, and cut into 1-inch wedges
1   cup thinly sliced onion
1   cup canned Italian plum tomatoes, well drained and coarsely chopped

1½ tablespoons minced fresh oregano or 1½ teaspoons crumbled dried oregano
½   teaspoon coarse salt
½   teaspoon freshly milled black pepper
4   teaspoons olive oil
2   tablespoons minced Italian parsley leaves, for garnish

1. Adjust oven rack to center of oven and preheat to 350° F.
2. Wash chicken legs and blot dry. Place legs on work surface. Starting at top of leg, slip your fingers under the skin to loosen. Peel off skin carefully, using a pair of kitchen shears to snip the skin

and any connecting membrane to avoid tearing the meat; discard skin. Trim off any membrane or bits of fat that may still be attached to leg.

3. Lightly grease bottom of a 9 × 13 × 2-inch ovenproof baking pan with cooking spray. Arrange drumsticks in single layer in pan. Arrange potatoes between and around drumsticks. Place a single layer of onion slices over drumsticks and potatoes. Spoon tomatoes over onions. Sprinkle oregano on top; season with salt and pepper. Drizzle with olive oil.

4. Cover pan with foil and bake for 25 minutes. Remove foil and baste with pan juices. Continue baking, basting frequently with pan juices, until drumsticks are very tender and potatoes are cooked, about 25 minutes.

5. Transfer drumsticks and potatoes to platter. Spoon tomatoes, onions, and pan juices over top. Garnish with parsley and serve.

PER SERVING: Cal. 349   Chol. 116 mg
              Fat 11 gm   Sod. 417 mg

~~~~~~

Braised Chicken Thighs with Tomato and Olives

[Pollo alla Cacciatora]

▦

SERVES 4

Even the heartiest of appetites will be satisfied with this flavorful Neapolitan hunter-style stew. Serve over individual portions of polenta.

Eight	5-ounce chicken thighs
½	cup Gold Medal Wondra flour
½	teaspoon freshly milled black pepper
1½	tablespoons olive oil
½	cup dry vermouth
1	medium red onion (6 ounces), peeled and thinly sliced
1	large red or green bell pepper (8 ounces), halved, cored, and thinly sliced
1	cup canned Italian plum tomatoes, coarsely chopped, juice included
1½	tablespoons minced fresh basil or 1½ teaspoons crumbled dried basil
2	large bay leaves
½	teaspoon coarse salt
¼	cup (about 12) oil-cured black olives, pitted and coarsely chopped

1. Wash chicken thighs in cold water and blot dry. Remove skin and any traces of fat and discard.
2. Combine flour and pepper in a shallow bowl. Dredge chicken thighs in seasoned flour and shake off excess (dredge just before cooking or coating will become gummy).
3. In a 10-inch sauté pan, heat oil over medium-high heat. Place all of the thighs in pan, skinned side down. Sauté until lightly golden on both sides; remove and set aside. Pour off all the pan drippings. Add vermouth, turn heat to high, and cook, scraping any fragments that might be stuck to bottom of pan, until liquid is reduced to half, about 3 minutes. Add onion and sliced pepper, turn

heat to medium, and cook, stirring constantly, until vegetables are barely tender, about 2 minutes. Add tomatoes, basil, and bay leaves; stir to incorporate.

4. Return chicken to pan and spoon most of the tomato mixture on top. Cover pan, turn heat to low, and cook, basting frequently, until the juices run clear when thighs are pierced with the tip of a small knife, about 30 minutes; season with salt.

5. Preheat oven to 200°F. Transfer chicken to an ovenproof platter and place in oven to keep warm, leaving sauce in pan.

6. Discard bay leaves and turn heat to high. Cook sauce, stirring constantly, until thickened, about 5 minutes. Stir in olives and cook for an additional minute. Pour sauce over chicken and serve.

PER SERVING: Cal. 334   Chol. 134 mg
              Fat 12 gm   Sod. 725 mg

Chicken Piccata

[Pollo Piccante]

SERVES 4

The piquant flavorings of vermouth, lemon, and thyme enliven this simple chicken sauté.

Four   5-ounce boneless, skinless chicken breast halves, well trimmed of fat
3   tablespoons Gold Medal Wondra flour
½   teaspoon freshly milled black pepper
2   tablespoons olive oil
½   cup dry vermouth

2   tablespoons strained lemon juice
½   teaspoon coarse salt
1   tablespoon minced fresh thyme or 1 teaspoon crumbled dried thyme
1   tablespoon freshly grated lemon rind

1. Place chicken breasts within a folded piece of plastic wrap; slightly flatten upper portion of each breast with the broad side of a chef's knife to promote even cooking.
2. On a piece of wax paper, combine flour and pepper. Lightly dredge each breast half in seasoned flour (dredge just before cooking or flour coating will become gummy).
3. In a 12-inch skillet, heat oil over medium-low heat. Add chicken and sauté until lightly golden, about 3 minutes on each side. Transfer to serving platter and cover loosely with a tent of foil.
4. Add the vermouth and lemon juice to skillet. Turn heat to medium and bring mixture to a boil, scraping any fragments left in bottom of pan with a wooden spoon. Season with salt and stir in thyme and lemon rind. Remove from heat, spoon sauce over chicken, and serve.

PER SERVING: Cal. 271   Chol. 82 mg
              Fat 9 gm   Sod. 278 mg

Chicken Breasts with Mushrooms and Sun-Dried Tomatoes

[Petti di Pollo con Funghi e Pomodoro Secco]

SERVES 4

The mushrooms and sun-dried tomatoes not only accentuate the flavoring of this dish but also keep the chicken quite moist.

¼ cup (about 10) sun-dried tomatoes, not packed in oil

Four 5-ounce boneless, skinless chicken breast halves, well trimmed of fat

3 tablespoons Gold Medal Wondra flour

½ teaspoon freshly milled black pepper

2 tablespoons olive oil

⅓ cup dry vermouth

½ cup thinly sliced shallots

8 ounces crimini or button mushrooms, wiped, trimmed, and thinly sliced

1 tablespoon minced fresh thyme or 1 teaspoon crumbled dried thyme

½ teaspoon coarse salt

1. Place tomatoes in small bowl. Pour on boiling water to cover and let stand 2 minutes to soften. Drain, blot dry, and slice into ¼-inch julienne strips; set aside.

2. Place chicken breasts within a folded piece of plastic wrap and slightly flatten upper portion of each breast with the broad side of a chef's knife to promote even cooking.

3. On a piece of wax paper, combine flour and pepper. Lightly dredge each breast half in seasoned flour (dredge just before cooking or flour coating will become gummy). In a 12-inch skillet, heat oil over medium heat. Add chicken and sauté until lightly golden, about 3 minutes on each side; transfer to plate.

4. Add vermouth to skillet, turn heat to low, and scrape any fragments left in bottom of pan with wooden spoon. Add shallots and cook until slightly softened, about 1 minute. Add mushrooms and

continue cooking, stirring constantly, for an additional minute. Stir in sun-dried tomatoes and thyme. Return chicken to pan and season with salt. Spoon a little mushroom mixture over chicken, cover pan, and cook an additional 2 minutes. Transfer chicken to platter, spoon remaining mushroom mixture on top, and serve.

PER SERVING: Cal. 303   Chol. 82 mg
Fat 9 gm   Sod. 287 mg

Roasted Chicken with Vinegar and Rosemary

[Pollo Arrostito con Aceto e Rosmarino]

SERVES 4

Plump whole fryers are wonderful for roasting. Basting frequently keeps the chicken tender and juicy. The skin is left on for presentation only—remember to slip it off before eating!

One 3-pound frying chicken, split in half and well trimmed of fat
⅓ cup white wine vinegar
1 tablespoon minced garlic
2 tablespoons minced fresh rosemary or 2 teaspoons crumbled dried rosemary

¾ cup Chicken Broth, preferably homemade (page 5), or defatted low-sodium canned
½ teaspoon coarse salt
½ teaspoon freshly milled black pepper
4 sprigs fresh rosemary, for garnish

1. Adjust oven rack to center of oven and preheat to 350°F. Place split chicken on a roasting rack in a shallow baking pan with skin side up; set aside.

2. In a small bowl, combine vinegar, garlic, and rosemary. Brush chicken with vinegar mixture. Place broth in bottom of roasting pan.

3. Roast chicken, basting with pan juices, until nicely browned and crisp, about 1 hour. Transfer chicken to platter and cut each section in half between breast and upper portion of leg. Cover with a tent of foil and set aside.

4. Spoon off any fat from roasting pan. Add 2 tablespoons water to pan and place over high heat, scraping any fragments left in bottom of pan with wooden spoon. Strain pan juices into bowl; season with salt and pepper. Spoon pan juices over chicken, garnish with rosemary, and serve. Remove skin before eating.

PER SERVING: Cal. 243 Chol. 108 mg
                      Fat 9 gm   Sod. 294 mg

~~~~~~

Warm Chicken Salad with Balsamic Dressing

[Insalata di Pollo Balsamico]

SERVES 4

A beautiful luncheon or light supper entrée. Crusty rolls and Tomato Salad with Zippy Ricotta Herb Dressing (page 154) are the perfect partners.

Four 5-ounce boneless, skinless chicken breast halves, well trimmed of fat

1 large bunch arugula (about 8 ounces), stems removed, thoroughly washed and spun dry

2 medium Belgian endive (about 6 ounces), halved lengthwise, cored, washed, spun dry, and sliced lengthwise into ½-inch strips

1 large red bell pepper (8 ounces), halved, cored, seeded and sliced lengthwise into ¼-inch strips

3 tablespoons Gold Medal Wondra flour

½ teaspoon coarse salt

½ teaspoon freshly milled black pepper

3 tablespoons extra virgin olive oil

½ cup thinly sliced scallions

2 tablespoons balsamic vinegar

1. Place chicken breasts within a folded piece of plastic wrap and slightly flatten upper portion of each breast with the broad side of a chef's knife to promote even cooking.

2. On 4 dinner plates, arrange leaves of arugula in a single layer. Place strips of Belgian endive lengthwise in a circular outer border on top of arugula. Place strips of red pepper lengthwise in between Belgian endive strips; set aside.

3. On a piece of wax paper, combine flour, salt, and pepper. Lightly dredge breast halves in seasoned flour.

4. In a 12-inch skillet, heat oil over medium-high heat. Sauté breast halves, turning once with metal spatula, until lightly golden, about

3 minutes on each side. Remove from pan and place chicken pieces on a cutting board. Slice the breast halves lengthwise at a slight angle into ½-inch strips. Arrange chicken slices in center of prepared plates.

5. Add scallions to pan and place over low heat. Cook for 30 seconds, stirring constantly. Add vinegar and stir to combine. Spoon warm dressing over each salad and serve.

PER SERVING: Cal. 266   Chol. 66 mg
Fat 12 gm   Sod. 284 mg

Roast Turkey Breast with Lemon Sauce

[Petto di Tacchino Arrostito con Salsa di Limone]

SERVES 6

Sweet Potatoes with Rosemary and Garlic (page 138) makes an admirable side dish to the sliced turkey breast.

One 3-pound fresh turkey breast, well trimmed of fat
1 large clove garlic, split in half
1 large lemon (3 ounces), cut in half crosswise
2 tablespoons minced fresh sage or 2 teaspoons crumbled dried sage
2½ cups Chicken Broth, preferably homemade (page 5), or defatted low-sodium canned

¼ cup strained lemon juice
2 teaspoons cornstarch
¼ cup cold water
½ teaspoon coarse salt
½ teaspoon freshly milled white pepper
1½ teaspoons grated lemon rind
1 tablespoon minced Italian parsley leaves
1 bunch curly parsley, for garnish

1. Adjust oven rack to center of oven and preheat to 400° F.
2. Rub entire surface of turkey breast with split garlic and discard garlic. Place turkey, skin side up, on rack in roasting pan. Rub cut lemon over turkey skin and then put the lemon halves on the rack under the breast. Sprinkle with sage. Pour 1½ cups broth over turkey, reserving remaining broth for sauce. Cover roasting pan with foil.
3. Roast breast in preheated oven for 30 minutes. Remove foil and lower oven temperature to 325° F. Baste turkey with pan juices every 20 minutes for an additional 1½ hours. Turkey is done when an instant-read thermometer inserted into the thickest portion of breast shows a reading of 165° F. Transfer breast to platter, cover loosely with foil, and let rest for ½ hour before carving.
4. Skim any surface fat from baking pan and discard. Add 3 table-spoons of the reserved broth to pan. Place over medium heat and scrape any fragments that might be stuck to bottom of pan. Pour pan juices through a strainer set over a small saucepan. Add remaining broth and strained lemon juice to saucepan. Cook over medium heat, stirring frequently, until slightly reduced, about 10 minutes.
5. Dissolve cornstarch in water and add to sauce. Turn heat to low and cook sauce, stirring constantly, until slightly thickened, about 5 minutes. Season with salt and pepper. Stir in lemon rind and Italian parsley; remove from heat.
6. Discard skin from turkey breast. Slice breast and arrange slices in an overlapping pattern on platter. Garnish with an outside border of curly parsley. Serve sauce separately.

PER SERVING: Cal. 209   Chol. 117 mg
Fat 1 gm   Sod. 213 mg

Grilled Turkey Tenderloins with Pimiento Sauce

[Tacchino Arrostito con Salsa di Pimento]

SERVES 6

Grilled turkey tenderloins are a nice change from chicken, especially during the summer months.

2 large scallions, washed, trimmed, and cut into 1-inch pieces to make ⅓ cup

One 6½-ounce jar pimientos, rinsed, well drained, and cut into 1-inch pieces

8 large fresh basil leaves or 1½ teaspoons crumbled dried basil

1½ tablespoons extra virgin olive oil

½ teaspoon coarse salt

½ teaspoon freshly milled black pepper

2 teaspoons minced garlic

½ cup strained lime juice

1½ tablespoons honey, preferably orange blossom

2 tablespoons minced fresh thyme or 2 teaspoons crumbled dried thyme

½ teaspoon cayenne pepper

Two ¾-pound turkey breast tenderloins, tendons removed

8 short sprigs fresh thyme, for garnish

1. Place scallions, pimientos, basil leaves, and olive oil in food processor. Process until sauce is a smooth purée, about 30 seconds. Transfer to small bowl. Season with salt and pepper; set aside. (Sauce can be prepared 2 days ahead, covered, and refrigerated until needed. Bring to room temperature before serving.)

2. In a low shallow bowl large enough to accommodate the turkey, combine garlic, lime juice, honey, thyme, and cayenne pepper. Place tenderloins in bowl and turn to coat with marinade. Cover with plastic wrap and refrigerate for at least 2 hours. Remove tenderloins from marinade, scraping any bits clinging to turkey back

into shallow bowl. Transfer marinade to small saucepan and bring to a boil; reserve.

3. Lightly grease grill rack with cooking spray. Preheat charcoal grill until coals have turned a gray ashy color or preheat gas grill according to manufacturer's suggested time on medium heat.

4. Place turkey on grill and cook 5 minutes, turning once. Brush with a little reserved marinade and continue grilling, turning frequently and basting with marinade, until turkey is cooked, about 12 minutes. Transfer to platter, tent with foil, and let rest for 5 minutes (this will make slicing easier). Slice turkey crosswise at a slight angle into ½-inch slices. Arrange on platter, garnish with thyme sprigs, and serve, offering pimiento sauce separately.

PER SERVING: Cal. 190   Chol. 70 mg
               Fat 4 gm   Sod. 187 mg

Peppers Stuffed with Ground Turkey

[Pepe Ripieni di Tacchino Macinato]

SERVES 4

This is a variation of my daughter, Joanne's, favorite stuffed pepper recipe, substituting low-fat ground turkey for the expected ground beef and pork.

¼ cup minced scallions

1 tablespoon minced fresh basil or 1 teaspoon crumbled dried basil

2 tablespoons minced Italian parsley leaves

½ teaspoon coarse salt

½ teaspoon freshly milled black pepper

1 cup fresh bread crumbs made from cubed Italian or French bread, including crust, coarsely ground in food processor or blender

1 large egg white, beaten

1 pound lean ground turkey

4 medium green bell peppers (1¾ pounds), washed, dried, halved vertically cored, and seeded

One 16-ounce can Italian plum tomatoes

8 teaspoons freshly grated imported Parmesan cheese

1. Adjust oven rack to center of oven and preheat to 350° F.
2. In a medium-size bowl, combine scallions, basil, parsley, salt, pepper, and bread crumbs. Stir in beaten egg white. Add turkey and mix well. Spoon stuffing into pepper halves and place in a 9 × 13 × 2-inch ovenproof baking dish.
3. Drain tomatoes in strainer set over a bowl, pressing lightly on tomatoes; reserve juice. Coarsely chop tomatoes and spoon over surface of peppers. Measure out ¾ cup of the reserved juice and pour into bottom of casserole.
4. Cover casserole with foil and bake in preheated oven for 35 minutes. Remove foil and continue baking, basting once with pan

juices, until peppers are tender, about 25 minutes. Remove from oven. Raise oven temperature to broil setting.

5. Spoon 1 teaspoon Parmesan cheese over each pepper half. Broil 4 inches from heat source until cheese is melted and tomatoes form a light crust on surface, about 2 minutes. Spoon a little of the pan juices over each pepper and serve.

PER SERVING: Cal. 289   Chol. 86 mg
                         Fat 10 gm   Sod. 641 mg

Turkey Cutlets with Marsala Wine Sauce

[Costoletta di Tacchino con Marsala]

SERVES 4

The versatility of turkey cutlets is really tested in this recipe. If you don't have dry marsala wine on hand, you may substitute a good dry sherry.

3   tablespoons Gold Medal Wondra flour
½   teaspoon freshly milled black pepper
Four   5-ounce turkey breast cutlets, each ¼ inch thick
2   tablespoons olive oil
½   cup thinly sliced scallions
1   teaspoon minced garlic

⅓   cup Chicken Broth, preferably homemade (page 5), or defatted low-sodium canned
⅓   cup dry marsala wine
½   teaspoon coarse salt
2   teaspoons minced fresh rosemary or ½ teaspoon crumbled dried rosemary
2   tablespoons minced Italian parsley leaves, for garnish

1. On a piece of wax paper, combine flour and pepper. Lightly dredge each cutlet in seasoned flour (dredge just before cooking or flour coating will become gummy).

2. In a 12-inch skillet, heat oil over medium-low heat. Add cutlets and sauté until lightly golden, about 2 minutes on each side. Transfer to platter.

3. Add scallions to skillet, turn heat to low, and cook, scraping any fragments left in bottom of pan with wooden spoon, until barely tender, about 2 minutes. Add garlic and sauté for 1 minute. Add chicken broth and wine to skillet. Turn heat to medium and cook until liquid is reduced to half, about 3 minutes. Season with salt and rosemary. Return cutlets and any accumulated juices to skillet. Spoon sauce over cutlets, turn heat to low, and simmer until heated, about 2 minutes. Transfer cutlets to platter. Spoon sauce over cutlets, garnish with parsley, and serve.

PER SERVING: Cal. 277   Chol. 87 mg
             Fat 8 gm   Sod. 260 mg

Fish and Seafood

Introduction

I learned early in life to view fish as a basic part of our weekly diet. I also learned at an early age to appreciate fish for its remarkable versatility. We ate fish every Friday, not only because we were Catholic, but because that was the day the fish was the freshest. My father always referred to fish as "brain food." Back in those days, many Americans didn't cook fish, didn't eat fish, and—for the most part—didn't like fish. If fish did appear on one's table, it was usually fried and served with tartar sauce. Shrimp was mainly served as shrimp cocktail, and squid, which sold for 25 cents a pound, was used for bait.

In the past decade, however, a remarkable change has taken place. The National Fishery Institute reports a marked increase in fish consumption. The reason for this increase is easy to understand. Low in fat and calories, high in protein and minerals, fish, as any nutritionist will tell you, should be part of a leaner, healthier diet. The increase in fish consumption may also be due to the greater variety and availability today.

Ease of preparation is another virtue, especially for the hurried cook. The recipes in this chapter will give you straightforward techniques that let the real flavor of the fish come through. With creative combinations of flavorings from herbs, wines, citrus juices, and vegetables, these dishes are relatively easy to prepare and can be delicious additions to your menu for anything from a simple family supper to an elegant and impressive company dinner.

Baked Fillet of Sole with Marjoram and Wine

[Pesce con Maggiorana e Vino]

▦

SERVES 6

Any thin, white-fleshed fish with a delicate flavor like gray or Dover sole may be substituted for the lemon sole—but make sure you purchase the freshest fish you can find.

½ cup finely chopped shallots
1 tablespoon minced fresh marjoram or 1 teaspoon crumbled dried marjoram
6 tablespoons dry bread crumbs
½ teaspoon coarse salt
½ teaspoon freshly milled black pepper

Six 5-ounce fillets of lemon sole
½ cup dry white wine
1½ tablespoons olive oil
3 tablespoons minced Italian parsley leaves, for garnish
1 large lemon, sliced into 6 wedges, for garnish

1. Adjust oven rack to upper portion of oven and preheat to 475°F. Lightly grease bottom of a 10 × 13 × 2-inch ovenproof baking pan with vegetable cooking spray. Sprinkle shallots in bottom of baking pan; set aside.
2. In a small bowl, combine marjoram, bread crumbs, salt, and pepper.
3. Rinse fillets under cold water and blot dry. Place fillets 1 inch apart in prepared pan. Pour wine over fillets. Spoon bread crumb mixture evenly over fillets and drizzle oil over top.
4. Bake in preheated oven until fish barely turns opaque, about 5 minutes. Remove from oven. Turn oven to broil setting. Broil fish 4 inches from heat source until lightly browned, about 2 minutes (watch carefully so that surface does not burn). Transfer fillets to platter and spoon pan juices over fish. Garnish with minced parsley and lemon wedges; serve immediately.

PER SERVING: Cal. 211   Chol. 68 mg
Fat 5 gm   Sod. 293 mg

Broiled Halibut Steaks with Tomato Caper Sauce

[Pesce con Salsa di Pomodoro e Capperi]

SERVES 6

In this dish, raw tomato sauce enlivened with herbs and capers complements succulent halibut steaks.

4 well-ripened plum tomatoes (½ pound), halved, cored, seeded, and cut into ¼-inch dice
¼ cup lightly packed minced Italian parsley leaves
¼ cup lightly packed minced fresh basil
1 teaspoon minced garlic
1½ tablespoons strained lemon juice

2 tablespoons nonpareil (small) capers, rinsed and drained
3 tablespoons olive oil
½ teaspoon coarse salt
½ teaspoon freshly milled black pepper
Six 6-ounce halibut steaks, each about 1 inch thick
1 large lemon, sliced into 6 wedges, for garnish

1. In a medium-size bowl, combine tomatoes, parsley, basil, garlic, lemon juice, capers, 1½ tablespoons of the olive oil, salt, and pepper. (Sauce can be prepared up to 2 hours before broiling fish. Cover with plastic wrap and leave at room temperature.)
2. Remove broiler rack and pan from oven; preheat oven on broil setting for 15 minutes. Lightly spray broiler rack with cooking spray; set aside.
3. Rinse halibut steaks under cold water and blot dry. Place steaks 2 inches apart on prepared pan and lightly brush them with remaining 1½ tablespoons of oil.
4. Broil steaks 4 inches from heat source without turning, just until fish is lightly golden on surface, about 5 minutes. When done, steaks should feel firm to the touch and barely flake when tested with the tip of a knife.

5. Transfer steaks to platter and spoon sauce over fish. Garnish with lemon wedges and serve.

PER SERVING: Cal. 226   Chol. 44 mg
                Fat 10 gm   Sod. 275 mg

Classic Squid Salad

[Insalata di Calamari]

SERVES 6

Boiling squid takes an extremely watchful eye. Start testing for tenderness after 90 seconds. Pull a piece of squid from skillet, dip it into ice water and taste. Squid can go from mushy to fairly tough in less than 2 minutes.

1½ pounds cleaned small squid
2   bay leaves, broken in half
5   tablespoons strained lemon juice
¼   cup diced peeled carrots (¼-inch dice)
½   cup thinly sliced celery, strings removed before slicing
¾   cup diced yellow bell pepper (½-inch dice)

⅓   cup minced red onion
½   teaspoon minced garlic
3   tablespoons minced Italian parsley leaves
½   teaspoon coarse salt
½   teaspoon freshly milled white pepper
2   tablespoons extra virgin olive oil

1. Thoroughly wash squid in cold water and blot dry. Slice body sacks crosswise into ¼-inch rings. Slice tentacles into 1-inch lengths.
2. In a 12-inch skillet, bring 3 cups water, bay leaves, and 3 table-spoons of the lemon juice to a boil. Add squid and cover skil-let. As soon as water returns to a boil, cook squid just until opaque, about 1 to 1½ minutes. Drain in colander, discard bay leaves, cool, and blot thoroughly dry.

3. Transfer squid to a deep bowl. Add carrots, celery, bell pepper, onion, garlic, and parsley; toss lightly.

4. Place salt, pepper, and remaining 2 tablespoons lemon juice in a small bowl. Add oil a little at a time and whisk until dressing is well blended. Pour dressing over salad; toss to combine. (Salad can be made up to 4 hours before serving. Cover with plastic wrap and refrigerate. Remove from refrigerator ½ hour before serving and toss again.)

PER SERVING: Cal. 157   Chol. 264 mg
              Fat 6 gm   Sod. 186 mg

Cod Steaks with Herbed Bread Crumbs

[Merluzzo con Erbe]

SERVES 4

The light coating of herbed bread crumbs over the surface of steaks prevents them from drying out while cooking at a high temperature.

2 teaspoons minced garlic

2 teaspoons minced fresh thyme or ½ teaspoon crumbled dried thyme

2 tablespoons snipped fresh chives or scallion tops

2 teaspoons finely grated lemon rind

½ teaspoon coarse salt

½ teaspoon freshly milled black pepper

½ cup well-packed fresh bread crumbs made from cubed Italian or French bread, including crust, coarsely ground in food processor or blender

1½ tablespoons olive oil

Four 6-ounce cod steaks, each ½ inch thick

2 tablespoons strained lemon juice

4 sprigs fresh thyme, for garnish

1. In a small bowl, combine garlic, thyme, chives, lemon rind, salt, pepper, and bread crumbs. Stir in oil and mix well; set aside.
2. Adjust oven rack to upper portion of oven and preheat to 450°F. Lightly grease bottom of a 9 × 13 × 2-inch baking pan with cooking spray.
3. Wash cod steaks in cold water and blot dry. Place steaks at least 2 inches apart in prepared pan and brush them with lemon juice. Carefully spoon bread crumb mixture over each steak, pressing lightly to adhere. (Try not to get any bread crumb mixture in bottom of pan; it will burn as fish cooks.)
4. Bake in preheated oven until fish barely flakes when tested with the tip of a knife, about 15 to 20 minutes. Transfer steaks to platter, garnish with fresh thyme, and serve.

PER SERVING: Cal. 227   Chol. 64 mg
              Fat 6 gm   Sod. 376 mg

Sea Bass Ligurian Style

[Branzino Liguriano]

SERVES 6

If sea bass is not available, fillets of red snapper or sea trout work extremely well in this recipe.

Six	5-ounce unskinned sea bass fillets	2	tablespoons minced fresh thyme or 2 teaspoons crumbled dried thyme
3	tablespoons dry vermouth	3	tablespoons strained fresh lemon juice
1½	tablespoons olive oil	3	tablespoons minced Italian parsley leaves, for garnish
½	teaspoon coarse salt		
½	teaspoon freshly milled black pepper		

1. Adjust oven rack to upper third of oven and preheat to 500°F. Lightly grease a 9 × 13 × 2-inch baking pan with cooking spray.
2. Wash fillets in cold water and blot dry. Place fillets in baking pan, skin side down.
3. Whisk vermouth and oil in a small bowl. Brush mixture over fillets. Season fish with salt and pepper and sprinkle thyme over fillets.
4. Bake fish in preheated oven for 4 minutes. Baste with pan juices and continue baking until fish barely flakes when tested with the tip of a knife in center, about 3 to 4 minutes. Transfer fish to platter; spoon pan juices over fish and sprinkle with lemon juice. Garnish with parsley and serve.

PER SERVING: Cal. 180   Chol. 58 mg
                 Fat 6 gm   Sod. 219 mg

Grilled Tuna with Orange Mint Dressing

[Tonno alla Genovese]

SERVES 6

This is one of my favorites to make during the summer months when yellowfin are running.

Three 10-ounce tuna steaks, each ¾ inch thick
2 tablespoons strained lemon juice
1 teaspoon minced garlic
3 tablespoons strained orange juice
½ teaspoon Dijon-style mustard
½ teaspoon sugar
½ teaspoon coarse salt
½ teaspoon freshly milled black pepper
2 tablespoons extra virgin olive oil
1½ tablespoons minced fresh mint or 1½ teaspoons crumbled dried mint
6 sprigs fresh mint, for garnish

1. Rinse tuna steaks in cold water and blot dry. Place them in a single layer in a shallow dish. Add lemon juice and garlic and turn steaks once to coat both sides thoroughly. Cover with plastic wrap and marinate in refrigerator for 1 to 2 hours.
2. Place orange juice, mustard, sugar, salt, and pepper in a small bowl. Whisk to combine. Add oil a little at a time and whisk until thoroughly blended. Stir in mint; set dressing aside.
3. Lightly grease grill rack with cooking spray. Preheat charcoal grill until coals have turned a gray ashy color, or preheat gas grill according to manufacturer's suggested time on high setting.
4. Remove steaks from marinade and blot dry. Discard marinade. Place steaks on grill and cook, covered with lid or tented with foil, for 3 minutes. Turn steaks and continue cooking, covered, until they are opaque and barely flake when tested with knife, about 4 minutes for rare and 5 minutes for medium.

5. Transfer tuna to serving platter and slice each steak in half. Whisk dressing once again and spoon over steaks. Garnish plate with sprigs of fresh mint and serve.

PER SERVING: Cal. 227   Chol. 47 mg
              Fat 10 gm   Sod. 184 mg

Herb-Crusted Salmon with Sun-Dried Tomato Sauce

[Salmone con Crosta di Erbe]

SERVES 4

Baked swordfish and halibut are also excellent with this sauce.

4   teaspoons olive oil
2   tablespoons minced shallots
1   tablespoon strained lemon juice
½   cup dry white wine
6   sun-dried tomatoes (not packed in oil), finely minced
½   teaspoon coarse salt
½   teaspoon freshly milled black pepper

1   tablespoon minced fresh basil or 1 teaspoon crumbled dried basil
1   tablespoon minced fresh thyme or 1 teaspoon crumbled dried thyme
2   teaspoons minced fresh rosemary or ½ teaspoon crumbled dried rosemary
½   cup dry bread crumbs
Two 12-ounce skinless salmon fillets

1. In a 10-inch nonstick skillet, heat 2 teaspoons oil over medium heat. Add shallots and sauté, stirring constantly, until lightly golden, about 1 minute. Add lemon juice, wine, and sun-dried tomatoes. Turn heat to medium-high and cook until sauce is reduced

to ½ cup, about 2 minutes. Season with salt and pepper and set aside. (Sauce can be made up to 1 hour before cooking fish. Reheat over low heat just before removing fish from oven.)

2. Adjust oven rack to center of oven and preheat to 400°F. Lightly grease a 9 × 13 × 2-inch ovenproof casserole with cooking spray; set aside.

3. On a piece of wax paper, combine basil, thyme, rosemary, and bread crumbs. Dredge each fillet in bread crumb mixture, coating well. Transfer fillets to prepared pan and place 2 inches apart. Drizzle with remaining 2 teaspoons oil.

4. Bake in preheated oven just until fish is opaque and barely flakes when tested in center with tip of knife, about 8 to 10 minutes. Transfer to serving platter, slice each fillet in half crosswise, spoon sauce over fillets, and serve.

PER SERVING: Cal. 376   Chol. 94 mg
                  Fat 16 gm   Sod. 360 mg

Shrimp with Spicy Tomato Sauce

[Gamberi con Pomodoro Piccante]

SERVES 6

For something a little different, try serving this Ligurian-style shrimp over Grilled Polenta, page 45.

2 pounds large shrimp, shelled and deveined
2 tablespoons olive oil
½ cup thinly sliced scallions
2 teaspoons minced garlic
One 16-ounce can Italian plum tomatoes, coarsely chopped, juice included

½ teaspoon coarse salt
½ teaspoon crushed red pepper flakes
½ teaspoon sugar
1 tablespoon grated lemon rind
3 tablespoons minced Italian parsley leaves, for garnish

1. Wash shrimp in cold water and drain in colander; set aside.
2. In a 12-inch skillet, heat oil over medium heat. Add scallions and sauté, stirring constantly, until tender-crisp, about 1 minute. Add garlic and cook for an additional minute. Stir in tomatoes, salt, pepper flakes, and sugar. Cook until sauce is slightly thickened and reduced to half, about 20 minutes. Stir in shrimp and cook, stirring frequently, just until they turn pink, about 2 to 3 minutes. Stir in lemon rind. Transfer to shallow bowl, garnish with parsley, and serve.

PER SERVING: Cal. 192   Chol. 186 mg
Fat 7 gm   Sod. 428 mg

Swordfish with Piquant Peppers

[Pesce Spada Agrodolce]

SERVES 4

The addition of a little sugar and vinegar to the peppers gives this fish a most succulent flavoring. Halibut or cod steaks may be substituted for the swordfish.

Two 10-ounce swordfish steaks, each ¾ inch thick

3 tablespoons Gold Medal Wondra flour

½ teaspoon freshly milled black pepper

2 tablespoons olive oil

1 cup thinly sliced red onion

1 large red pepper (8 ounces), halved, cored, seeded, and sliced into ¼-inch strips

1 large yellow pepper (8 ounces), halved, cored, seeded, and sliced into ¼-inch strips

¼ cup white wine vinegar

1 tablespoon sugar

1 tablespoon minced fresh sage or 1 teaspoon crumbled dried sage

½ teaspoon coarse salt

4 sprigs fresh sage, for garnish

1. Wash steaks under cold water and blot dry.
2. On a piece of wax paper, combine flour and pepper. Dredge steaks in seasoned flour and shake off excess. (Dredge just before cooking so coating will not get gummy.)
3. In a 12-inch skillet, heat 1 tablespoon oil over medium heat. Add steaks and sauté 1 minute on each side. Transfer steaks to a platter.
4. Add remaining oil to skillet; turn heat to low. Stir in onion and cook, stirring constantly, scraping bottom of pan to loosen any fragments that might be stuck. Add peppers and cook until barely tender, about 2 minutes. Stir in vinegar, sugar, and sage. Return

steaks to pan and spoon some of the vegetable mixture on top. Cook, partially covered, until steaks are opaque and barely flake when tested with tip of knife, about 3 minutes. Season with salt and remove from heat. Transfer steaks to platter and slice each in half vertically. Spoon remaining vegetable mixture over each portion. Garnish with sage and serve.

PER SERVING: Cal. 290   Chol. 49 mg
                    Fat 12 gm   Sod. 303 mg

Vegetables

Introduction

Vegetables play a major role in the Italian menu. With the freshest seasonal varieties available at our markets today, there is no reason for them to take a minor role on our plates. Here is one place you can feel free to indulge.

One of my favorite methods of preparation, especially with broccoli, green beans, or zucchini, is to steam them until tender-crisp, rub a bowl with split garlic, and quickly toss them with a little extra virgin olive oil, a light sprinkling of salt or lemon juice, and lots of freshly milled black pepper. Served at room temperature, this is truly the Italian way—seasonal and simple.

Quite often after a satisfying dish of pasta, polenta, or risotto, I serve leafy green vegetables such as broccoli di rape, escarole, swiss chard, kale, or spinach as a second course rather than a salad.

The recipes that follow spotlight vegetables. However, they also play a vital part in many of the recipes that make up Lean Italian Cooking. Never left waiting in the wings, they take a strong supporting role in the soups, pasta, polenta, rice, and pizza recipes and share top billing along with meats, poultry, and fish entrées.

Braised Broccoli di Rape

[Broccoli di Rape Saltate]

SERVES 6

In some markets, broccoli di rape is called rapini. Select bunches with firm, small stems and bright green buds. It is most plentiful from late fall to spring.

2 pounds broccoli di rape	½ teaspoon coarse salt
2½ tablespoons olive oil	½ teaspoon crushed red pepper
3 large cloves garlic, peeled and quartered	flakes

1. Remove any discolored leaves from broccoli di rape. Cut off about ½ inch of tough bottom stems. Cut off florets about 3 inches from top. Using a small paring knife and starting at the bottom, peel stems and cut them into 3-inch lengths. Wash several times in lukewarm water to remove sand and drain thoroughly in colander.

2. In a large 5-quart dutch oven, heat oil over medium-high heat. Add garlic, turn heat to low, and cook until very lightly golden. Remove from heat and place broccoli di rape in pan. Cook, covered, over medium-high heat until stems are barely tender, about 5 minutes. Uncover pan, turn heat to high, and continue to cook until stems are extremely tender and very little liquid is left in bottom of pan, about 2 minutes. Season with salt and crushed red pepper flakes. Remove garlic, transfer to platter, and serve. Broccoli di rape is also delicious served lukewarm.

PER SERVING: Cal. 87   Chol. 0 mg
              Fat 6 gm   Sod. 183 mg

~~~~~~

Broccoli with Olives and Sage

[Broccoli e Olive]

SERVES 6

This truly flavorful combination is best served at room temperature.

1 large bunch broccoli (2½ pounds)
2½ tablespoons extra virgin olive oil
1 teaspoon finely minced garlic
¼ cup medium-size (about 8) oil-cured black olives, pitted and thinly sliced

1 tablespoon minced fresh sage or 1 teaspoon crumbled dried sage
½ teaspoon coarse salt
½ teaspoon freshly milled black pepper

1. Wash broccoli and drain well. Remove and discard any large coarse leaves; cut off about 1 inch of tough lower part of stalks. Peel stalks with a vegetable peeler. If stalks are large, cut lengthwise into halves or quarters. Cook broccoli in 4 quarts boiling water until stalks are tender, about 7 minutes. Drain in a colander, refresh under cold water, and blot dry.
2. In a 12-inch skillet, heat oil over low heat. Sauté garlic, stirring constantly, until very lightly golden, about 1 minute. Stir in olives and sauté, stirring constantly, until they puff a little, about 1 minute. Add sage and broccoli; cook until broccoli is warmed through. Season with salt and pepper. Transfer to platter and serve, either hot or at room temperature.

PER SERVING: Cal. 120   Chol. 0 mg
              Fat 8 gm   Sod. 365 mg

~~~~~~

Broccoli with Roasted Peppers and Pine Nuts

[Broccoli e Pepe Arostiti con Pignoli]

SERVES 6

The texture and color of the broccoli florets contrast beautifully with the roasted peppers in this tasty and attractive dish.

5 cups bite-size pieces broccoli florets, with ½ inch of stems included, washed and drained

2½ tablespoons extra virgin olive oil

3 tablespoons minced shallots

2 large firm red bell peppers (1 pound), roasted, peeled, and sliced into ½-inch strips (see page 135 for roasting techniques)

½ teaspoon coarse salt

½ teaspoon freshly milled black pepper

3 tablespoons pine nuts, lightly toasted

1. Cook florets in 4 quarts of boiling water until barely tender, about 3 minutes. Drain in a colander, refresh under cold water, and blot dry.
2. In a 12-inch skillet, heat oil over low heat. Sauté shallots, stirring constantly, until very lightly golden, about 2 minutes. Add florets and roasted peppers; cook until vegetables are warmed through. Season with salt and pepper. Transfer to platter and garnish with toasted pine nuts.

PER SERVING: Cal. 120   Chol. 0 mg
                Fat 8 gm   Sod. 144 mg

Brussels Sprouts and Baby Carrots

[Cavoli di Brusselle e Carote]

SERVES 4

Try to select brussels sprouts of uniform size for this delightful fall combination.

1 pound (1 pint) brussels sprouts

½ pound baby carrots, washed, trimmed, and cut into 2-inch lengths

2 tablespoons extra virgin olive oil

¼ cup minced shallots

1 tablespoon strained lemon juice

½ teaspoon coarse salt

½ teaspoon freshly milled black pepper

2 tablespoons minced Italian parsley leaves

1. Wash brussels sprouts, trim off tough outer leaves, and cut a shallow cross in the bottom of each. Cook brussels sprouts in 2 quarts boiling water until tender, about 8 minutes. Transfer to colander, refresh under cold water, and blot dry; set aside.
2. Cook carrots in 1 quart boiling water until tender, about 4 minutes. Transfer to colander, refresh under cold water, and blot dry.
3. In a 10-inch skillet, heat oil over medium heat. Add shallots, turn heat to low, and sauté until soft and lightly golden, about 2 minutes. Add vegetables and cook, stirring constantly until heated through, about 2 minutes. Stir in lemon juice; season with salt and pepper. Remove from heat and stir in parsley. Transfer to small platter and serve.

PER SERVING: Cal. 135   Chol. 0 mg
　　　　　　　 Fat 7 gm   Sod. 229 mg

Cauliflower with Herbed Bread Crumbs

[Cavolfiore alla Mama]

SERVES 4

The lightly sautéed garlic and herbed bread crumbs combined with the cauliflower make an unforgettable vegetable for late fall or winter.

1 small head cauliflower (about 1¼ pounds)	3 tablespoons dry bread crumbs
2 teaspoons minced fresh thyme or ½ teaspoon crumbled dried thyme	2 tablespoons extra virgin olive oil
2 teaspoons minced fresh basil or ½ teaspoon crumbled dried basil	2 teaspoons minced garlic
	½ teaspoon coarse salt
	½ teaspoon freshly milled black pepper
1 tablespoon minced Italian parsley leaves	

1. Remove florets from cauliflower, leaving about ½ inch of stems. Cut or break florets into 1-inch pieces. Wash in cold water and drain. Cook florets in 2 quarts boiling water until tender, about 7 minutes. Transfer to colander and drain well.
2. In a small bowl, combine thyme, basil, parsley, and bread crumbs; set aside.
3. In a 10-inch skillet, heat oil over low heat. Add garlic and sauté, stirring constantly until very lightly golden, about 2 minutes. Add cauliflower and toss with garlic mixture until heated, about 2 minutes. Season with salt and pepper. Stir in bread crumb mixture and cook, stirring and tossing constantly, until cauliflower is coated with crumb mixture, about 30 seconds. Remove from heat, transfer to bowl, and serve.

PER SERVING: Cal. 96   Chol. .23 mg
              Fat 7 gm   Sod. 227 mg

Eggplant Sandwiches

[Melanzane Involtini]

▣

SERVES 4

Be sure to pick 2 eggplants of matching shape so that when sandwiched, they will be the same size in this substantial, delicious, meatless main course.

1½ cups Light Tomato Sauce (page 19)
2 tablespoons olive oil
2 medium eggplants (about 1½ pounds)
8 slices low-fat Swiss cheese (4 ounces)
⅓ cup Gold Medal Wondra flour
½ teaspoon coarse salt

½ teaspoon freshly milled black pepper
1 large egg
1 large egg white
1½ cups dry bread crumbs
2 tablespoons minced fresh basil or 2 teaspoons crumbled dried basil
2 tablespoons minced Italian parsley leaves

1. Prepare the light tomato sauce up to 4 hours before cooking eggplant sandwiches.
2. Adjust oven rack to upper portion of oven and preheat to 375°F. Line a jelly roll pan with parchment paper and lightly brush with 2 teaspoons oil.
3. Wash and dry eggplants. Trim off both ends and discard. Slice each eggplant into eight ½-inch-thick rounds.
4. Fold each slice of cheese into quarters and place them in center of 8 eggplant slices, leaving a border of eggplant showing. Top each with another eggplant slice.
5. On a piece of wax paper, combine flour, salt, and pepper. In a shallow bowl, lightly beat egg, egg white, and 3 tablespoons cold water. On another piece of wax paper, combine bread crumbs, basil, and parsley. Dredge sandwiches in flour mixture, dip into egg mixture, and firmly press each side in seasoned bread crumbs. Place the eggplant sandwiches 2 inches apart in prepared pan. Drizzle ½ teaspoon oil over each sandwich. Bake in preheated

oven until underside is lightly golden, about 12 minutes. Remove from oven and turn sandwiches over. Continue baking until underside is golden and eggplant is tender, about 10 minutes.

6. Heat tomato sauce in a small saucepan. Transfer 2 sandwiches to each dinner plate. Spoon 1 heaping tablespoon of sauce on each sandwich and serve remaining sauce on the side.

PER SERVING: Cal. 455   Chol. 81 mg
              Fat 18 gm   Sod. 799 mg

Sautéed Eggplant with Green Pepper and Tomato

[Melanzane Saltata]

SERVES 4

Select glossy, firm eggplant for this very simple but tasty dish.

2 tablespoons olive oil
½ cup finely chopped scallions
1 medium green pepper
   (5 ounces), halved, cored,
   seeded, and finely chopped
3 well-ripened plum
   tomatoes (8 ounces),
   blanched, peeled, cored, and
   coarsely chopped
1 medium eggplant (about 12
   ounces), washed, ends
   trimmed, peeled, and cut into
   1-inch cubes

½ teaspoon coarse salt
½ teaspoon freshly milled
   black pepper
2 tablespoons minced fresh basil
   or 2 teaspoons crumbled
   dried basil
2 tablespoons minced Italian
   parsley leaves

In a 12-inch skillet, heat oil over low heat. Add scallions and green pepper; cook until pepper is barely tender, about 3 minutes. Stir in tomatoes; turn heat to medium. Cook, stirring and mashing a few tomatoes with the back of a wooden spoon, for 2 minutes. Add eggplant cubes and cook until barely tender, about 3 minutes. Season with salt and pepper. Stir in basil and cook for another minute. Stir in parsley and remove from heat. Transfer to platter and serve.

PER SERVING: Cal. 103   Chol. 0 mg
             Fat 7 gm   Sod. 193 mg

Escarole with Raisins and Pine Nuts

[Scarola alla Lucchesi]

SERVES 4

A good vegetable dish for winter, when escarole is abundant. This can be prepared up to 3 hours before serving, but omit raisins and pine nuts. Reheat over low heat, with raisins and stir in pine nuts just before serving.

2 medium heads escarole (about 2 pounds)
2 tablespoons extra virgin olive oil
3 medium cloves garlic, peeled and sliced in half

½ teaspoon coarse salt
½ teaspoon freshly milled black pepper
¼ cup dark raisins
2 tablespoons pine nuts, lightly toasted

1. Discard any wilted or bruised leaves from escarole. Separate leaves and cut off tough bottom ends (about 1 inch), and discard. Slice greens into 1-inch lengths. Wash several times in lukewarm water to remove sand; thoroughly drain in colander.
2. In a deep 5-quart dutch oven, heat oil over low heat. Add garlic and sauté until lightly golden. Remove pan from heat; discard gar-

lic with slotted spoon. Place escarole in pan and cover. Cook over moderately low heat until escarole is tender, about 8 to 10 minutes. Remove cover, turn heat to high, and cook until very little liquid is left in bottom of pan, about 2 minutes. Season with salt and pepper and stir in raisins. Cook until raisins are plumped, about 30 seconds. Stir in toasted pine nuts, transfer to bowl, and serve.

PER SERVING: Cal. 147   Chol. 0 mg
               Fat 9 gm   Sod. 228 mg

Green Beans with Sun-Dried Tomatoes

[Fagiolini Verdi con Pomodoro Secco]

SERVES 4

Italians are known to serve many vegetables at room temperature. This one is an excellent dish that can be assembled ahead of time.

¼ cup sun-dried tomatoes (not packed in oil)

1¼ pounds green beans, washed and bottoms trimmed

2 tablespoons extra virgin olive oil

¼ cup minced red onion

1 tablespoon minced fresh basil or 1 teaspoon crumbled dried basil

½ teaspoon coarse salt

½ teaspoon freshly milled black pepper

1. Place sun-dried tomatoes in a small bowl. Pour boiling water to cover tomatoes and let stand 2 minutes to soften. Drain, blot dry, and slice into ¼-inch strips; set aside.
2. Cook green beans in 2 quarts boiling water until barely tender, about 4 minutes. Drain in colander; rinse under cold water. Blot dry and cut diagonally into 2-inch lengths.

3. In a 12-inch skillet, heat oil over low heat. Add onions and cook, stirring frequently, until barely softened, about 1 minute. Add green beans and sun-dried tomatoes; continue cooking, stirring frequently, until green beans are heated through, about 2 minutes. Stir in basil; season with salt and pepper and remove from heat. Transfer to platter and serve either hot or at room temperature.

PER SERVING: Cal. 113   Chol. 0 mg
              Fat 7 gm   Sod. 196 mg

Jerusalem Artichokes and Peas

[Topinambur e Piselli]

SERVES 4

Jerusalem artichokes, also known as sunchokes, have a slightly sweet flavor. Once you've tried this simple recipe, accented with the flavoring of fennel seed, it may become a regular in your repertoire. Just keep an eye on the chokes so that they don't overcook and become mushy.

½ pound Jerusalem artichokes (sunchokes)
2 tablespoons extra virgin olive oil
½ cup thinly sliced scallions

One 9-ounce package tiny frozen peas, defrosted and well drained
½ teaspoon crushed fennel seed
½ teaspoon coarse salt
½ teaspoon freshly milled black pepper

1. With a vegetable peeler, remove thin outer skin from each artichoke. Thoroughly wash several times in cold water, drain, and

blot dry. (Chokes will turn a light beige color after cleaning.) Slice each in half crosswise and then lengthwise into ¼-inch strips.

2. In a deep 3½-quart saucepan, heat oil over medium heat. Add scallions, turn heat to low, and cook until softened but not brown, about 2 minutes. Stir in artichokes, cover pan, and cook just until tender-crisp, about 5 to 8 minutes. Stir in peas and fennel. Cook for an additional 3 minutes. Season with salt and pepper. Transfer to bowl and serve.

PER SERVING: Cal. 138   Chol. 0 mg
              Fat 7 gm   Sod. 271 mg

Braised Kale and Kidney Beans

[Cavolo Riccio e Fagioli]

SERVES 6

Select small deep green colored kale bunches with slightly moist leaves. It is most flavorful and abundant during the winter months. This hearty dish is on my menu quite often during the winter season.

1½	pounds kale	One	16-ounce can dark red kidney beans, rinsed and well drained
2	tablespoons olive oil		
1	cup thinly sliced onions		
1	cup carrots, cut in ½-inch dice	½	teaspoon coarse salt
		½	teaspoon freshly milled black pepper

1. Kale leaves should always be stripped from their stems. Either hold the stem with one hand and pull the leaves off with the other hand or run a knife along each side to free the leaves. Wash several times in lukewarm water. Remove from final rinse water and place

in a large 6-quart pot. Do not add water; there will be enough clinging to the leaves. Cover pot and bring to a boil. Uncover pot and boil vigorously, stirring down leaves once or twice, until kale is tender. (Small leaf kale may take about 4 to 5 minutes; large leaf kale will take a little longer.) Thoroughly drain in colander. When cool enough to handle, cut kale into 1-inch strips and set aside.

2.   In a deep 4-quart saucepan, heat oil over low heat. Sauté onion and carrots until slightly softened, about 6 minutes. Add kale and cook until very tender. Stir in beans, salt, and pepper; cook an additional 5 minutes, partially covered. (This dish can be prepared up to 3 hours before serving. Reheat over low heat, partially covered.)

PER SERVING: Cal. 146   Chol. 0 mg
              Fat 5 gm   Sod. 253 mg

Technique for
Roasting Peppers

When large thick-skinned bell peppers are available, buy several pounds.
Roast the peppers, peel, and leave in large strips. Place in plastic containers
and freeze until needed. Defrost peppers 4 hours or overnight in
refrigerator before using.

Select large firm red, yellow, or green bell peppers for roasting. Look over each pepper carefully to be sure it has no blemishes. For perfect roasting, each pepper should weigh at least 6 to 8 ounces.

1. Adjust oven rack to 6 inches from broiler and preheat to broil setting.
2. Wash peppers in cold water; blot dry with paper towel. Slice off both ends of each pepper to make a cylinder. Discard top and bottom ends or save for another use. Cut each half lengthwise into 3 even pieces. Lay the pepper pieces on work surface with skin side down. Carefully remove all seeds and slice off any protruding ribs.
3. Place pepper strips, cut side down, on a baking sheet. Broil peppers until partially charred, about 5 minutes. Remove from oven, wrap in paper towels, and place in a plastic bag. Secure the end with a twist tie and let stand for at least 1 hour to cool. Remove from bag and peel peppers with a small paring knife. Pat dry with paper towel and cut into desired lengths.

Roasted New Potatoes

[Patate Arostiti]

◼

SERVES 4

*Be sure to use a baking pan large enough to hold the potatoes in a single
layer so they will roast properly and not steam.*

2 pounds small new potatoes,
all the same size

2 teaspoons minced garlic

½ teaspoon coarse salt

¼ teaspoon crushed red
pepper flakes

1 tablespoon fresh thyme or 1
teaspoon crumbled dried
thyme

2 tablespoons olive oil

2 tablespoons minced Italian
parsley leaves, for garnish

1. Scrub potatoes well with a vegetable brush. Trim and discard ends
and quarter the potatoes. Cook, covered, in a steamer with one
inch of water in bottom of pan, until barely tender, about 4 minutes. (The skins stay more intact in a steamer than in boiling water.) Remove from steamer and let cool to room temperature.
Place potatoes between layers of paper towel and blot thoroughly
dry.

2. Adjust oven rack to upper portion of oven and preheat to 425°F.

3. In shallow 2-quart baking pan, combine all the remaining ingredients except parsley. Place potatoes in pan and toss to coat.

4. Bake in preheated oven, turning potatoes once or twice with metal
spatula, until golden brown and tender, about 20 minutes.

5. Transfer to platter, garnish with parsley, and serve.

PER SERVING: Cal. 247   Chol. 0 mg
                      Fat 7 gm   Sod. 201 mg

Stewed Potatoes and Zucchini in Tomato Sauce

[Giambotta]

SERVES 6

Giambotta is an Italian vegetable stew. Vegetables can vary according to the season or the mood of the cook. Cut green beans or cubed eggplant may be substituted for the zucchini.

1½ tablespoons olive oil
1 cup thinly sliced onion
One 16-ounce can peeled tomatoes, coarsely chopped, juice included
½ teaspoon coarse salt
½ teaspoon freshly milled black pepper
½ teaspoon sugar
3 large red-skinned potatoes (1 pound), scrubbed, ends trimmed, and cut into 1½-inch dice

4 medium zucchini (1 pound), scrubbed, ends trimmed, and cut into ½-inch rounds
2 tablespoons minced fresh basil or 2 teaspoons crumbled dried basil
2 tablespoons minced Italian parsley leaves

1. In a heavy 5-quart dutch oven, heat oil over medium heat. Add onion and cook, stirring frequently, until lightly golden. Stir in tomatoes, salt, pepper, and sugar. Turn heat to high and cook sauce, stirring once or twice, for 10 minutes. Add potatoes, turn heat to low, cover pan, and cook until potatoes are barely tender, about 10 minutes.
2. Stir in zucchini and basil; cook, covered, until zucchini is tender-crisp, about 10 minutes. Stir in parsley, transfer to bowl, and serve.

PER SERVING: Cal. 129   Chol. 0 mg
              Fat 4 gm   Sod. 254 mg

Sweet Potatoes with Rosemary and Garlic

[Patate Dolce con Rosmarino e Aglio]

SERVES 6

These flavorful oven-roasted potatoes go extremely well with any of the roasted poultry recipes in this book.

4 large sweet potatoes
  (about 3½ pounds)
2 tablespoons minced fresh
  rosemary or 2 teaspoons
  crumbled dried rosemary

2 tablespoons minced garlic
½ teaspoon coarse salt
½ teaspoon freshly milled
  black pepper
2½ tablespoons extra virgin olive
  oil

1. Scrub potatoes well with a vegetable brush. Place them in a 6-quart pot with enough water to cover by 2 inches. Cover pot, bring to a boil, and cook until potatoes are barely tender, about 15 minutes. Transfer to a colander and let stand until cool enough to handle. Peel skins with a small paring knife. Slice about 1 inch from each end of each potato and discard. Slice potatoes into 1-inch rounds.
2. Adjust oven rack to center of oven and preheat to 450°F. Lightly grease the bottom of a large jelly roll pan with vegetable cooking spray. Arrange potato slices in a single layer, spacing about 1 inch apart.
3. Using a fork, combine remaining ingredients in a small bowl. Spoon about ½ teaspoon of mixture on top of each round and spread evenly with a narrow metal spatula. Bake until potatoes are tender and slightly crusty on top, about 35 minutes. Transfer to platter and serve immediately.

PER SERVING: Cal. 257   Chol. 0 mg
              Fat 6 gm   Sod. 148 mg

Spinach with Lemon

[Spinaci con Limone]

SERVES 4

Lightly season with garlic and lemon to add a pungent accent to the spinach.

2¼ pounds young tender spinach
2 tablespoons extra virgin olive oil
2 cloves garlic, split in half
½ teaspoon coarse salt
½ teaspoon freshly milled black pepper
1 tablespoon grated lemon rind

1. Cut off and discard spinach stems and any limp leaves. Wash spinach several times in tepid water to remove sand. Drain in colander; set aside.
2. In a 5-quart dutch oven, heat oil over medium-low heat. Add garlic and sauté until very lightly golden. Remove from heat and discard garlic.
3. Place spinach in pan. Cover with lid and cook over medium heat until spinach is wilted, about 3 minutes. Uncover pan, turn heat to high, and continue cooking, stirring frequently, until spinach is tender and very little liquid is left in bottom of pan, about 2 minutes. Season with salt and pepper; stir in lemon rind. Transfer to bowl and serve.

PER SERVING: Cal. 105   Chol. 0 mg
Fat 7 gm   Sod. 328 mg

Swiss Chard with Tomatoes

[Bietole Saltate]

SERVES 4

Choose crisp-stalked bunches with firm bright leaves. The peak of the season for Swiss chard is May through October. This is a simple way to prepare either green or ruby Swiss chard.

2 pounds Swiss chard
2 tablespoons olive oil
1 cup thinly sliced onion
3 well-ripened plum
   tomatoes (8 ounces),
   blanched, peeled, and coarsely
   chopped

½ teaspoon coarse salt
½ teaspoon freshly milled black
   pepper

1. Trim off any wilted or discolored edges from chard leaves and cut leaves from stems. Trim bottom of stems. Wash leaves and stems separately in tepid water several times to get rid of sand; drain well. Slice stems diagonally about ½ inch wide. (If stems are wider than 1 inch, lightly peel with a vegetable peeler to remove fibrous strings.) Slice leaves crosswise into 2-inch lengths.

2. In a heavy 5-quart saucepan, heat oil over low heat. Add onion and cook until barely tender, about 2 minutes. Stir in tomatoes and chard stems. Cover and cook over low heat, stirring frequently, about 15 to 25 minutes. Add chard leaves and stir to combine. Cover and cook over medium heat, stirring once or twice, until tender, about 10 minutes. Uncover pan, turn up heat, and cook until very little liquid is left in bottom of pan, about 2 to 3 minutes. Season with salt and pepper, transfer to bowl, and serve.

PER SERVING: Cal. 124   Chol. 0 mg
               Fat 7 gm   Sod. 612 mg

Broiled Tomatoes

[Pomodori Arrostiti]

SERVES 4

A good side dish to make during late summer when tomatoes are at their peak.

2 tablespoons plus 1 teaspoon extra virgin olive oil

2 large well-ripened tomatoes (12 ounces), washed, cored, and halved crosswise

½ teaspoon coarse salt

½ teaspoon freshly milled black pepper

1 tablespoon minced shallots

½ cup fresh bread crumbs made from cubed Italian or French bread, including crust, coarsely ground in food processor or blender

1 tablespoon minced fresh basil or 1 teaspoon crumbled dried basil

1. Lightly grease bottom of an 8 × 8 × 2-inch ovenproof baking dish with 1 teaspoon oil. Place tomato halves in prepared dish, cut sides up, and season them with salt and pepper.
2. In a small nonstick skillet, heat remaining 2 tablespoons oil over low heat. Add shallots and sauté, stirring constantly, until soft but not brown. Add bread crumbs and basil; mix with fork until combined. Remove from heat and spoon bread crumb mixture evenly over tomatoes. (Tomatoes can be prepared 1 hour ahead. Let stand at room temperature.)
3. Preheat oven to broil setting. Set baking dish 4 to 5 inches from heat source and broil tomatoes until crumbs are brown and crisp and tomatoes are just warmed through, about 3 minutes. (Watch carefully so crumbs do not burn.) Transfer to platter and serve.

PER SERVING: Cal. 109   Chol. .06 mg
Fat 6 gm   Sod. 237 mg

Grilled Zucchini

[Zucchini Arrostiti]

◫

SERVES 4

For best flavor, serve at room temperature with any of the grilled poultry, meat, or fish dishes in this book.

4 medium-size zucchini (1 pound)
1 tablespoon extra virgin olive oil
1 tablespoon balsamic vinegar
½ teaspoon coarse salt

½ teaspoon freshly milled black pepper
1 tablespoon minced fresh oregano or 1 teaspoon crumbled dried oregano

1. Scrub zucchini under cold running water until the skins feel clean and smooth. Cook whole, unpeeled zucchini in 2 quarts boiling water until barely tender, about 2 minutes. Drain in colander, refresh under cold water, and blot dry. Trim ends of zucchini and slice each in half lengthwise.

2. Lightly grease grill rack with vegetable oil or cooking spray. Preheat charcoal grill until coals have turned a gray ashy color. Preheat gas grill according to manufacturer's suggested time on medium-high heat.

3. Lightly brush cut surface of zucchini with olive oil. Place on grill, cut side down. Grill zucchini until cut surface is lightly golden, about 2 minutes. Transfer to platter and arrange in single layer with grilled side up. Lightly sprinkle with balsamic vinegar, season with salt and pepper, sprinkle with oregano, and serve. (This dish is also excellent served at room temperature.)

PER SERVING: Cal. 47   Chol. 0 mg
              Fat 3 gm   Sod. 187 mg

Salads

Introduction

Italians traditionally serve an uncomplicated green salad either with or after the meal. These salads are usually made with a selection of fresh seasonal greens: romaine, escarole, curly chicory, arugula, young dandelions, endive, and an assortment of leaf lettuces. The mixed greens are lightly dressed with a splash of either balsamic or imported red wine vinegar, seasoned with salt and freshly milled black pepper, and then lightly tossed with a fruity extra virgin olive oil.

Whether I offer salad with a meal or after a meal, I insist on serving it on a separate plate so that the delicate dressing will not mingle with the entrée.

In addition to the typical salads of garden-fresh greens, a number of salad recipes incorporating vegetables and fruits follow. More substantial salads that serve as satisfying main courses appear in the chapters on pasta, rice, poultry, and seafood.

~~~~~~

Arugula and Radicchio Salad with Parsley Dressing

[Insalata alla Franci]

▦

SERVES 4

The distinctive flavors of arugula and radicchio need only the lightest of dressings.

3 tablespoons minced Italian leaf parsley
¼ cup minced red onion
½ teaspoon sugar
½ teaspoon coarse salt
½ teaspoon freshly milled black pepper
1 tablespoon balsamic vinegar
2½ tablespoons extra virgin olive oil

2 bunches arugula, stems discarded, thoroughly washed, spun dry, and cut into bite-size pieces to make about 3 cups
1 small head radicchio (about 5 ounces), halved, cored, leaves separated, washed, spun dry, and cut into bite-size pieces
1 cup thinly sliced celery, strings removed before slicing

1. In a small bowl, place parsley, onion, sugar, salt, pepper, and vinegar; stir with a fork or small whisk to combine. Add oil, a little at a time, whisking until dressing is well blended.
2. In a salad bowl, combine arugula, radicchio, and celery. Drizzle the dressing over and toss salad gently until it is well combined.

PER SERVING: Cal. 94   Chol. 0 mg
              Fat 9 gm   Sod. 223 mg

Asparagus Salad with Sun-Dried Tomato Vinaigrette

[Insalata di Asparagi]

SERVES 4

The sun-dried tomato and garlic dressing enhances the flavor of asparagus and turns it into exotic fare.

2 pounds medium-size asparagus
6 sun-dried tomatoes (not packed in oil)
½ teaspoon minced garlic
½ teaspoon coarse salt

½ teaspoon freshly milled black pepper
1 tablespoon balsamic vinegar
2½ tablespoons extra virgin olive oil
1 tablespoon minced fresh basil leaves

1. Cut off tough part at base of each asparagus spear and wash spears in cold water to get rid of sand. With a vegetable peeler, peel up from base of spears, leaving tips intact. Trim stalks so they are all the same length.
2. In a deep 12-inch skillet, bring 1½ quarts of water to a boil. Place asparagus in one or two layers in pan (they should be covered with water). Boil uncovered until stalks are tender but not limp when tested with the tip of a knife, about 4 to 7 minutes. Drain in colander, refresh under cold water, and blot dry. Transfer to flat plate, cover with plastic wrap, and refrigerate until needed.
3. Place sun-dried tomatoes in a small bowl, cover with boiling water, and let stand 2 minutes to soften. Drain, blot dry, and mince finely.
4. Place the tomatoes, garlic, salt, pepper, and vinegar in a small bowl; stir with fork to combine. Add oil, a little at a time, whisking until dressing is well blended; stir in basil.
5. Arrange asparagus on 4 salad plates, spoon dressing over each portion, and serve.

PER SERVING: Cal. 116   Chol. 0mg
              Fat 9 gm   Sod. 191 mg

Beet and Radicchio Salad

[Insalata di Barbabietola e Radicchio]

SERVES 4

In selecting fresh beets, try to choose those that are no more than 2 inches in diameter; larger ones tend to be fibrous. If radicchio is unavailable, you may substitute 2 cups shredded red cabbage.

1 small red onion (2 ounces), peeled and sliced paper-thin
1¼ pounds (5 or 6) medium-size beets
1 medium head radicchio (about 6 ounces), halved, cored, leaves separated, washed, spun dry, and cut into thin julienne strips

1½ tablespoons minced fresh mint leaves
½ teaspoon coarse salt
½ teaspoon freshly milled black pepper
1 tablespoon red wine vinegar
2½ tablespoons extra virgin olive oil

1. Place sliced onions in a small bowl with 3 ice cubes and cover with cold water. Refrigerate for at least 1 hour. (Soaking the onion will ensure crispness.)
2. Wash and trim beets, leaving 2 inches of the stems and the root ends intact to prevent color from oozing out during boiling. Place in a medium-size pot and cover with water; cover pot and bring to a boil. Cook beets, partially covered, over high heat until tender when pierced with a metal cake tester, about 20 to 40 minutes. Drain in colander and let cool until you can slip off the skins; slice off the stems. Quarter beets and cut into ½-inch wedges.
3. Drain onion, blot dry with paper towel, and combine with beets. Arrange in center of serving platter and surround with julienned strips of radicchio.
4. In a small bowl, combine mint, salt, pepper, and vinegar; stir with fork or small whisk to combine. Add oil, a little at a time, whisking until dressing is well combined. Spoon dressing over salad and serve.

PER SERVING: Cal. 129   Chol. 0 mg
Fat 9 gm   Sod. 256 mg

~~~~~~

Bibb, Watercress, Cucumber, and Radish Salad

[Insalata di Latuga, Crescione, Cetriolo, e Ravanello]

SERVES 6

A good salad to serve from late fall through the winter months, when all of these vegetables are readily available.

1 tablespoon minced shallots
½ teaspoon coarse salt
½ teaspoon freshly milled black pepper
½ teaspoon honey, preferably orange blossom
2 tablespoons strained lemon juice
2½ tablespoons extra virgin olive oil
5 cups loosely packed Bibb lettuce leaves (2 medium heads), rinsed, spun dry, and torn into bite-size pieces

1 bunch watercress (6 ounces), coarse stems discarded, rinsed and spun dry
1 large cucumber, peeled, halved lengthwise, seeds removed with a melon baller, thinly sliced to make 1 cup
8 large radishes, washed, trimmed, and sliced paper-thin to make ½ cup
1 tablespoon snipped fresh basil leaves

1. Place shallots, salt, pepper, honey, and lemon juice in a small bowl; stir with fork or small whisk to combine. Add oil, a little at a time, whisking until dressing is well blended.
2. In a salad bowl, toss together Bibb lettuce, watercress, cucumber, radishes, and basil. Drizzle dressing over salad and toss gently until well combined.

PER SERVING: Cal. 72   Chol. 0 mg
               Fat 6 gm   Sod. 142 mg

Cauliflower
and Roasted Pepper Salad

[Insalata di Cavolfiore e Pepe Arrostiti]

▨

SERVES 6

Adding the cauliflower to the dressing while still warm will bring out the full flavor of this salad. The roasted peppers are added to the cooled salad to prevent the cauliflower from turning pink.

1 medium head cauliflower (1½ pounds)
½ teaspoon coarse salt
½ teaspoon sugar
3 teaspoons imported white wine vinegar
1 teaspoon minced garlic
½ teaspoon freshly milled white pepper

2½ tablespoons extra virgin olive oil
2 large firm red bell peppers (1 pound), roasted, peeled, and sliced into ½-inch strips (see page 135, for roasting technique)
3 tablespoons minced Italian parsley leaves

1. Cut cauliflower into medium-size florets, leaving about ½ inch of stem. Trim heavy skin from stems. Cook cauliflower in 4 quarts boiling water until tender, about 10 minutes. Drain in colander, refresh briefly under cold water, and blot dry.
2. While cauliflower is cooking, make dressing. Place salt and sugar in deep bowl and pour in vinegar. Stir until salt and sugar are dissolved (this is best done with your index finger so that you can feel when the salt and sugar have dissolved). Add garlic and pepper; whisk in olive oil. Add cauliflower to dressing and mix well. Cover with plastic wrap and marinate at room temperature for at least 1 hour.
3. Just before serving, toss cauliflower with roasted peppers and parsley. Transfer to platter and serve.

PER SERVING: Cal. 80   Chol. 0 mg
               Fat 6 gm   Sod. 130 mg

Green Bean and New Potato Salad

[Insalata di Fagiolini Verdi e Patate]

SERVES 6

Steam the potatoes rather than boil them for this salad to keep the skins intact and make a more attractive presentation when combined with tender green beans.

1½ pounds small red-skinned potatoes	3 tablespoons extra virgin olive oil
½ teaspoon coarse salt	¼ cup minced red onion
½ teaspoon freshly milled white pepper	1 pound green beans, washed and trimmed
2 tablespoons imported white wine vinegar	3 tablespoons minced Italian parsley leaves

1. Scrub potatoes well with a vegetable brush. Trim off and discard ends and cut potatoes into 1-inch dice. In a steamer with 1 inch of water in bottom of pan, cook potatoes, covered, until tender, about 5 to 7 minutes. (Cooking them in a steamer will keep the skins intact better than boiling in water.)

2. While potatoes are cooking, make dressing. In the same bowl in which you are serving salad, combine salt, pepper, and vinegar; stir with fork or small whisk to combine. Add oil, a little at a time, whisking until dressing is well blended. Stir in minced onion; set aside.

4. As soon as potatoes are cooked, transfer to bowl with dressing. (This must be done while the potatoes are still hot so they will absorb the full flavor of the dressing.)

5. Cook beans in 2 quarts boiling water until tender-crisp, about 5 to 7 minutes. Drain in colander and rinse under cold water. Blot dry and cut diagonally into 2-inch lengths. Gently toss beans and parsley with potatoes. (Salad can be prepared up to 2 hours before serving. Cover with plastic wrap and let stand at room temperature. Gently toss again before serving.)

PER SERVING: Cal. 176   Chol. 0 mg
               Fat 7 gm   Sod. 136 mg

Mixed Greens and Pear Salad with Scallion Dressing

[Insalata Mista con Pera]

SERVES 4

Although this salad should be tossed with the dressing at the very last minute, the vinaigrette can be made up to 2 hours ahead of time.

¼ cup finely chopped scallions

½ teaspoon sugar

½ teaspoon coarse salt

½ teaspoon freshly milled black pepper

1 tablespoon balsamic vinegar

2½ tablespoons extra virgin olive oil

4 cups torn bite-size pieces romaine lettuce, bottom trimmed, leaves washed and spun dry before tearing

1 large head Belgian endive (3 ounces), halved lengthwise, cored, washed, spun dry, and sliced into ½-inch widths

½ cup thinly sliced celery, strings removed before slicing

2 tablespoons minced Italian parsley leaves

1 large well-ripened Bosc pear

1. Place scallions, sugar, salt, pepper, and balsamic vinegar in a small bowl; stir with fork or small whisk to combine. Add oil, a little at a time, whisking until dressing is well blended.

2. In a salad bowl, toss together the romaine, endive, celery, and parsley. Wash, halve, stem, and core the pear, cut it into ½-inch dice, and add to the greens. Drizzle dressing over salad and toss gently until well combined.

PER SERVING: Cal. 125   Chol. 0 mg
              Fat 9 gm   Sod. 203 mg

~~~~~~

Orange and Fennel Salad

[Insalata d'Aranci e Finocchio]

▦

SERVES 4

This artfully arranged salad is as good to eat as it is beautiful to look at and will complement any fish dish in this book.

4 large navel oranges
(2½ pounds)
1 large fennel bulb with
leaves (about 1 pound
weighed with 2 inches of
leaves)
½ teaspoon sugar

¼ cup minced red onion
½ teaspoon coarse salt
½ teaspoon freshly milled white
pepper
2 tablespoons extra virgin olive
oil

1. Cut a slice from top and bottom of each orange to expose the fruit. Peel the oranges and remove all the white membrane with a vegetable peeler. Slice crosswise into ¼-inch rounds. Place in strainer set over a bowl to drain thoroughly for at least 30 minutes; reserve ⅓ cup juice for dressing.
2. Remove small feathery leaves from top of fennel stalks, finely chop, and reserve ¼ cup for garnish. Cut off upper stalks of bulb and discard. Trim base of bulb and, with a vegetable peeler, lightly peel outside of bulb to remove strings. Slice bulb in half vertically and remove center core with a V-cut. Slice fennel thinly into 1½-inch strips.
3. On a flat platter, arrange orange slices in a circular outer border with slices slightly overlapping. Arrange sliced fennel in the same manner in center of platter.
4. In a small bowl, place reserved juice, sugar, onion, salt, and pepper. Stir with fork to combine. Add oil, a little at a time, whisking until dressing is well blended.
5. Spoon dressing over salad and garnish with chopped fennel leaves.

PER SERVING: Cal. 171   Chol. 0 mg
Fat 7 gm   Sod. 277 mg

Roasted Pepper Salad

[Insalata di Pepe Arrostiti]

SERVES 4

For best flavor, make this salad one day in advance. If there's any left over, it makes for a wonderful sandwich on a crispy Italian roll.

2 large firm red bell peppers (1 pound), roasted, peeled, and sliced into ½-inch strips (see page 135 for roasting technique)
2 large firm yellow bell peppers (1 pound), roasted, peeled, and sliced into ½-inch strips
2 teaspoons balsamic vinegar

1 teaspoon minced garlic
1 tablespoon minced fresh oregano or 1 teaspoon crumbled dried oregano
½ teaspoon coarse salt
½ teaspoon freshly milled black pepper
2½ tablespoons extra virgin olive oil
2 large heads Belgian endive (8 ounces)

1. In a medium bowl combine pepper strips; set aside.
2. Place vinegar, garlic, oregano, salt, and pepper in a small bowl. Add oil and whisk to combine. Pour dressing over peppers, cover with plastic wrap, and let marinate at room temperature for 1 hour. (Peppers can be prepared 1 day in advance. Cover with plastic wrap, refrigerate, and return to room temperature 1 hour before serving.)
3. When ready to serve, trim bottom core of Belgian endive; carefully remove leaves and wipe with a damp cloth. On a serving plate, arrange an outer border of endive leaves and spoon roasted pepper salad in center.

PER SERVING: Cal. 136   Chol. 0 mg
              Fat 9 gm   Sod. 191 mg

~~~~~~

Tomato Salad with
Zippy Ricotta Herb Dressing

[Pomodoro all Cristina]

▓

SERVES 6

This creamy dressing spiked with a little horseradish is a perfect foil for well-ripened tomatoes.

⅓ cup part-skim ricotta
¼ cup 1% low-fat milk
1½ teaspoons prepared horseradish
2 tablespoons minced basil leaves
1 tablespoon snipped fresh chives
1 tablespoon minced Italian parsley leaves

½ teaspoon coarse salt
½ teaspoon freshly milled white pepper
4 large ripe tomatoes (about 2 pounds)
2 large clusters fresh basil sprigs, for garnish

1. Place ricotta, milk, and horseradish in a small deep bowl. With a wire whisk, mix until creamy. Add basil, chives, parsley, salt, and pepper; whisk again to combine. (Dressing can be made 4 hours ahead. Cover with plastic wrap and refrigerate until needed.)
2. Wash and dry tomatoes. Core and slice into ¼-inch rounds, discarding first and last slice. Arrange slices on platter in a slightly overlapping circular pattern. Spoon dressing over tomatoes and garnish center with fresh basil sprigs.

PER SERVING: Cal. 58   Chol. 4 mg
              Fat 2 gm   Sod. 158 mg

Pizza and Focaccia

Introduction

Pizza as Americans have come to know and love it from calling their local pizzerias seems an unlikely addition to a book dedicated to lean Italian cooking. With its incredibly thick crust, sodium-saturated sauce, fat-filled cheese, and greasy, additive-laden processed pepperoni and pork sausage, pizza would appear to provide a catastrophic combination of cholesterol and calories.

Consider, if you will, pizzas redesigned for today's healthier life-style, still tasty but nutritionally lower in calories and fat. With the substitution of part-skim ricotta and low-fat mozzarella, and by steaming, sautéing, and roasting a wide assortment of popular vegetables and seasoning with fresh herbs, pizza leaps lightly into the nineties.

The key to any great pizza is the crust. If you are a serious pizza maker, I would suggest that you purchase a large 18-inch-square pizza stone about ½ inch thick and follow the manufacturer's directions for using it. This will produce a crust like ones traditionally baked in brick ovens. However, the home baker can still make exceptional pizza crust by using a large baking sheet set on the lowest shelf of a 500°F. oven that has been preheated for at least 30 minutes. When weather permits, you may want to try your hand at pizza on the grill. This method guarantees the crispiest crust, one that can only be compared to pizzas baked in brick ovens. The techniques for grilling pizzas appear on page 167.

The pizzas in this chapter are ideal for individual portions. You will find them a lot easier to handle, especially if you have never made pizza before. If, however, you prefer one large pizza, each recipe will yield one 15-inch round. Now, I hope, you won't automatically reach for the phone and place your order, but try making any one of the varieties in this chapter. Once again you'll realize nothing beats homemade!

Focaccia is a rustic flat bread, similar to pizza but lighter in texture because the dough has two risings. It is lightly coated with extra virgin olive oil and delicately dressed with onion or garlic and fresh herbs.

An excellent accompaniment to any of the soup, meat, poultry, or fish dishes in this book, it can be eaten hot from the oven, warm, or at room temperature. It's perfect to take on picnics or cut into small squares and serve with a glass of wine before dinner.

Pizza Dough

MAKES ENOUGH DOUGH
FOR FOUR 6½-INCH ROUND
PIZZA CRUSTS

½ teaspoon sugar
1 cup lukewarm water, 105°
to 115°F.
One ¼-ounce package active dry
yeast
1 tablespoon olive oil

2 to 2½ cups bread flour or
unbleached all-purpose
flour
½ teaspoon coarse salt
½ teaspoon olive oil, for
coating bowl

In a 2-cup glass measure, stir sugar into water. Sprinkle yeast over water and stir briefly until completely dissolved. Set aside until foamy, about 5 minutes. Add 1 tablespoon oil and whisk to combine.

FOOD PROCESSOR METHOD: Place 2 cups plus 2 tablespoons flour and the salt in food processor and process for 15 seconds to combine. With machine running, slowly pour dissolved yeast mixture through feed tube and process for 50 seconds. (Dough will form a mass and is kneaded by spinning in machine for this period of time.) At this point, dough should feel slightly sticky. If dough feels wet, gradually add reserved flour, 1 tablespoon at a time; process for 5 seconds after each addition until dough reaches desired consistency. Transfer dough to lightly floured surface and knead until it is smooth and satiny, about 2 minutes. Shape dough into a ball.

ELECTRIC MIXER METHOD: In bowl of heavy-duty electric mixer fitted with flat paddle attachment, place 1¾ cups flour and salt; run machine at low speed for 20 seconds to combine. Add yeast mixture and run machine on medium speed until dough starts to pull together in a sticky mass. Scrape dough from paddle attachment into bowl. Remove paddle attachment and insert dough hook. Add additional flour, 2 tablespoons at a time, and run machine on medium speed until dough is

~~~~~~

kneaded into a soft mass that pulls away from sides of bowl, about 3 minutes. Transfer dough to a lightly floured surface and knead until smooth and satiny, about 5 minutes. Shape dough into a ball.

HAND METHOD: In a deep bowl, place 1½ cups flour and salt; stir to combine. Stir in yeast mixture and beat with wooden spoon until blended. Gradually stir in additional flour, ¼ cup at a time, until mixture forms a ball that cleans the sides of bowl. Transfer to lightly floured surface and knead dough, adding additional flour as needed, until smooth and satiny, about 8 to 10 minutes. Shape dough into a ball.

Lightly grease bottom and sides of a deep 2½-quart bowl with ½ teaspoon oil. Place dough in greased bowl, turning ball to coat entire surface with oil. Cover tightly with plastic wrap and let rise in a draft-free area until doubled in size, about 60 to 70 minutes. Punch risen dough down in center. Transfer to a lightly floured surface and divide dough into 4 equal pieces. Knead each piece briefly. Reshape into 4 balls, place on platter spaced 2 inches apart, and cover with dish towel. Let dough rest for 20 minutes so gluten mesh will relax a little, making it easier to shape or roll. Dough is now ready to be shaped, topped, and cooked.

PER CRUST: Cal. 320   Chol. 0 mg
              Fat 5 gm   Sod. 185 mg

Mushroom and Sun-Dried Tomato Pizzas

[Pizza di Funghi e Pomodoro Secco]

MAKES 4 INDIVIDUAL PIZZAS

The earthy flavoring of dry porcini mushrooms is a nice balance when combined with the button mushrooms and sun-dried tomatoes for this pizza topping. Dried thyme may be substituted, but is not quite as aromatic and fresh.

1 recipe Pizza Dough (page 158)
½ ounce dried porcini mushrooms
⅓ cup thinly sliced shallots
12 ounces fresh button mushrooms, wiped and thinly sliced
6 large sun-dried tomatoes (not packed in oil), sliced lengthwise into ¼-inch strips

1 tablespoon minced fresh thyme or 1 teaspoon crumbled dried thyme
½ teaspoon coarse salt
½ teaspoon freshly milled black pepper
4 teaspoons olive oil
¼ cup minced Italian parsley leaves, for garnish

1. Prepare pizza dough and shape into 4 balls, as instructed.
2. Adjust oven rack one shelf up from bottom of oven and preheat to 500°F. for 30 minutes.
3. Soak dried mushrooms in 1 cup lukewarm water for 30 minutes. Drain mushrooms in strainer over a bowl; reserve liquid. Pour liquid through strainer lined with paper towel to remove sand; set aside. Rinse mushrooms in cold water, blot dry, coarsely chop, and set aside. In a 12-inch skillet, heat ½ cup of the reserved mushroom liquid over high heat. Add shallots and cook, stirring frequently, until softened. Add fresh mushrooms and cook just until tender, about 1 minute. Stir in dried mushrooms and sun-dried tomatoes. Continue cooking, stirring frequently, until sun-dried tomatoes are softened and no liquid is left in bottom of pan, about

2 minutes. Stir in thyme and season with salt and pepper; remove
from heat.

4. Lightly grease a 14 × 16-inch baking sheet with cooking spray.
5. Place 1 ball of dough on well-floured work surface (keep remain-
    ing dough covered with a towel as you work). With the palm of
    your hand, flatten dough into a round disk. Flip dough over and
    use fingertips or rolling pin to shape or roll into a 6½-inch circle,
    lifting and turning dough clockwise as you shape or roll to stretch
    it gently. Place on prepared baking sheet. Repeat with remaining
    dough, spacing rounds ½ inch apart on sheet.
7. Lightly brush each round with 1 teaspoon olive oil. Spoon mush-
    room mixture over each round.
8. Bake until bottoms are crisp and edges are golden brown, about
    20 to 25 minutes. Transfer to cutting board and sprinkle with
    parsley. Slice each pizza into quarters and serve.

PER PIZZA: Cal. 423   Chol. 0 mg
              Fat 10 gm   Sod. 384 mg

~~~~~~

Red Onion, Fresh Tomato, Mozzarella, and Basil Pizzas

[Pizza di Liguria]

◼

MAKES 4 INDIVIDUAL PIZZAS

This is my favorite pizza because of its simplicity. Round, well-ripened tomatoes may be substituted for the plum tomatoes during the summer months. This is one that I make on the grill quite often during the summer.

1 recipe Pizza Dough (page 158)
1 cup thinly sliced red onion
⅓ cup Chicken Broth, preferably homemade (page 5), or defatted low-sodium canned
4 teaspoons olive oil
4 large well-ripened plum tomatoes (12 ounces), ends trimmed, sliced into ¼-inch rounds

½ teaspoon coarse salt
½ teaspoon freshly milled black pepper
1 cup grated part-skim mozzarella cheese (4 ounces)
¼ cup fresh basil leaves, sliced into thin strips

1. Prepare pizza dough and shape into 4 balls, as instructed.
2. Adjust oven rack one shelf up from bottom of oven and preheat to 500°F. for 30 minutes.
3. In a 10-inch nonstick skillet, cook onion in chicken broth over medium heat until liquid has completely evaporated and onions are lightly golden, about 4 minutes; remove from heat.
4. Lightly grease a 14 × 16-inch baking sheet with cooking spray.
5. Place 1 ball of dough on well-floured work surface (keep remaining dough covered with towel as you work). With the palm of your hand, flatten into a round disk. Flip dough over and use fingertips or rolling pin to shape or roll into a 6½-inch circle, lifting and turning dough clockwise as you shape or roll to stretch it gently. Place on prepared baking sheet. Repeat with remaining dough, spacing rounds ½ inch apart on sheet.

6. Lightly brush surface of each round with 1 teaspoon olive oil. Sprinkle onions over each to within ¼ inch of outside rim of dough. Place tomatoes in a circular pattern over onions. Season with salt and pepper. Sprinkle ¼ cup mozzarella cheese over each pizza.

7. Bake until bottoms are crisp and edges are golden brown, about 20 to 25 minutes. Transfer to cutting board and sprinkle basil over pizzas. Slice each pizza into quarters and serve.

PER PIZZA: Cal. 471   Chol. 16 mg
               Fat 15 gm   Sod. 516 mg

Ricotta, Broccoli, and Sage Pizzas
[Pizza di Ricotta, Broccoli, e Salvia]

MAKES 4 INDIVIDUAL PIZZAS

This Tuscan-style pizza is very moist and flavorful with just a hint of red pepper. The Roasted Pepper Salad on page 153 is an excellent accompaniment.

1 recipe Pizza Dough (page 158)

4 cups bite-size pieces broccoli florets with ½ inch of stem included, washed and drained

4 teaspoons olive oil

1 cup part-skim ricotta cheese

½ teaspoon coarse salt

½ teaspoon crushed red pepper flakes

1 tablespoon minced fresh sage or 1 teaspoon crumbled dried sage

1. Prepare pizza dough and shape into 4 balls, as instructed.

2. Adjust oven rack one shelf up from bottom of oven and preheat to 500°F. for 30 minutes.

3. Cook florets in 2 cups boiling water until barely tender, about 3 minutes. Drain in colander; set aside.

4. Lightly grease a 14 × 16-inch baking sheet with cooking spray.

5. Place 1 ball of dough on well-floured work surface (keep remaining dough covered with towel as you work). With the palm of your hand, flatten into a round disk. Flip dough over and use fingertips or rolling pin to shape or roll into a 6½-inch circle, lifting and turning dough clockwise as you shape or roll to stretch it gently. Place on prepared baking sheet. Repeat with remaining dough, spacing rounds ½ inch apart on sheet.

6. Lightly brush surface of each round with 1 teaspoon olive oil. Spread ¼ cup ricotta over each round to within ¼ inch of outside rim of dough. Arrange florets over each round. Sprinkle salt, pepper flakes, and sage over each pizza.

7. Bake until bottoms are crisp and edges are golden brown, about 20 to 25 minutes. Transfer to cutting board, slice each pizza into quarters, and serve.

PER PIZZA: Cal. 487   Chol. 19 mg
            Fat 15 gm   Sod. 476 mg

~~~~~~

Zucchini and Roasted Pepper Pizzas

[Pizza di Zucchini e Peppe Arrostiti]

▓

MAKES 4 INDIVIDUAL PIZZAS

The sweetness of the roasted bell peppers combined with zucchini and rosemary add special flavoring to this version.

1 recipe Pizza Dough (page 158)
4 medium zucchini (1 pound), well scrubbed
4 teaspoons olive oil
1 cup thinly sliced scallions
2 large red bell peppers (1 pound), roasted, peeled, and sliced into ¼-inch strips (see page 135 for roasting technique)

½ teaspoon coarse salt
½ teaspoon freshly milled black pepper
1 tablespoon minced rosemary or 1 teaspoon crumbled dried rosemary
4 teaspoons freshly grated imported Parmesan cheese

1. Prepare pizza dough and shape into 4 balls, as instructed.
2. Adjust oven rack one shelf up from bottom of oven and preheat to 500°F. for 30 minutes.
3. Cook whole zucchini in 1 quart boiling water until barely tender, about 3 minutes. Drain in colander, refresh under cold water, and blot dry. Trim ends of zucchini and slice into ¼-inch rounds; set aside.
4. Lightly grease a 14 × 16-inch baking sheet with cooking spray.
5. Place 1 ball of dough on well-floured work surface (keep remaining dough covered with towel as you work). With the palm of your hand, flatten into a round disk. Flip dough over and use fingertips or rolling pin to shape or roll into a 6½-inch circle, lifting and turning dough clockwise as you shape or roll to stretch it gently. Place on prepared baking sheet. Repeat with remaining dough, spacing rounds ½ inch apart on sheet.

6. Lightly brush each round with 1 teaspoon olive oil. Sprinkle ¼ cup scallions over each round to within ¼ inch of outside rim of dough. Place zucchini slices in a circular pattern over scallions. Arrange roasted pepper strips over zucchini. Sprinkle salt, pepper, rosemary, and 1 teaspoon Parmesan cheese over each pizza.
7. Bake until bottoms are crisp and edges are golden brown, about 20 to 25 minutes. Transfer to cutting board, slice each pizza into quarters, and serve.

PER PIZZA: Cal. 421   Chol. 2 mg
                   Fat 10 gm   Sod. 416 mg

Technique for
Cooking Pizza on the Grill

Grilled pizza has gained great popularity in the United States over the last few years. Pizza prepared in this manner produces a particularly crisp crust and can be ready to serve in less than 10 minutes. In order to save both steps and time, I recommend organizing all ingredients and cooking tools within easy reach before starting to grill. The procedure for cooking pizza on the grill is a little different from the traditional oven method. You will be working with 2 pieces of dough at a time. One side of the dough is lightly cooked, flipped over, and then dressed with the pizza topping of your choice. Rounds are then returned to the grill to finish cooking. Follow these simple steps and you will produce a perfect grilled pizza.

1. Prepare 1 recipe of Pizza Dough (page 158), and shape into 4 balls, as instructed.
2. Prepare any one of the pizza toppings on preceding pages. Place all ingredients in separate bowls on a tray along with wide metal spatula, brush, and spoons.
3. Adjust grill racks on either charcoal or gas grill to highest setting. Lightly grease grill racks with cooking spray. Preheat lidded charcoal grill until coals have turned a gray ashy color. Preheat gas grill according to manufacturer's suggested time on medium heat.
4. Lightly grease 2 baking sheets with cooking spray. Follow directions in Step 5 of each recipe for shaping pizza rounds. Place 2 rounds of dough on each prepared sheet, spacing them 4 inches apart. Cover each with a sheet of aluminum foil that has been lightly sprayed with cooking spray.
5. Lightly dust a cutting board with 3 tablespoons of cornmeal to prevent pizza from sticking when being flipped.
6. Working with 2 rounds of dough at a time, place on grill. Cover with lid and cook until underside forms a very lightly golden crust, about 2 to 3 minutes, rotating clockwise with wide metal spatula every 30 seconds to prevent any burned spots. Flip pizza rounds *grilled side up* onto prepared cutting board. Brush grilled rounds with amount of olive oil suggested and half of the pizza

toppings, making sure that toppings are placed to within ¼ inch of outside rim so they won't fall off and burn. Slide back onto grill with metal spatula and cook, covered, until bottoms are crisp and edges are golden brown, about 3 to 4 minutes. To avoid burned spots on bottom crust, give pizza a quarter turn with spatula every 30 to 40 seconds. Transfer to a clean dry cutting board and either garnish or cut according to recipe. Repeat with remaining 2 rounds of dough. (Check cutting board on which pizza was flipped, dusting with additional cornmeal as needed.)

~~~~~~

Focaccia Dough

▦

MAKES ENOUGH DOUGH FOR ONE
10 × 15-INCH FOCACCIA
YIELDING 24 SLICES

1	teaspoon sugar	3	to 3½ cups unbleached all-purpose flour
1¼	cups lukewarm water, 105° to 115°F.	½	teaspoon coarse salt
One	¼-ounce package active dry yeast	½	teaspoon olive oil, for coating bowl
1½	tablespoons olive oil		

In a 2-cup glass measure, stir sugar into water. Sprinkle yeast over water and stir briefly until completely dissolved. Set aside until foamy, about 5 minutes. Add 1½ tablespoons oil and whisk to combine.

FOOD PROCESSOR METHOD: Place 3 cups flour and salt in food processor and process for 15 seconds to combine. With machine running, slowly pour dissolved yeast mixture through feed tube and process for 50 seconds. (Dough will form a mass and is kneaded by spinning in machine for this period of time.) At this point, dough should feel slightly sticky. If dough feels wet, gradually add reserved flour, 1 tablespoon at a time; process for 5 seconds after each addition until dough reaches desired consistency. Transfer dough to lightly floured surface and knead until it is smooth and satiny, about 2 minutes. Shape into ball.

ELECTRIC MIXER METHOD: In bowl of heavy-duty electric mixer fitted with flat paddle attachment, place 2½ cups flour and salt; run machine at low speed for 20 seconds to combine. Add yeast mixture and run machine on medium speed until dough starts to pull together in a sticky mass. Scrape dough from paddle attachment into bowl. Remove paddle attachment and insert dough hook. Add additional flour, 2 tablespoons at a time, and run machine on medium speed until dough is kneaded into a soft mass that pulls away from sides of bowl, about 3 minutes. Transfer dough to a lightly floured surface and knead until smooth and satiny, about 5 minutes. Shape dough into a ball.

HAND METHOD: In a deep bowl, place 2 cups flour and salt; stir to combine. Stir in yeast mixture and beat with wooden spoon until blended. Gradually stir in additional flour, ¼ cup at a time, until mixture forms a ball that cleans the sides of bowl. Transfer to lightly floured surface and knead, adding additional flour as needed, until dough is smooth and satiny, about 8 to 10 minutes. Shape into a ball.

Lightly grease bottom and sides of a deep 3-quart bowl with ½ teaspoon oil. Place dough in greased bowl, turning ball to coat entire surface with oil. Cover tightly with plastic wrap and let rise in a draft-free area until doubled in size, about 60 to 70 minutes. Punch risen dough down in center. Gently pull the outside edges of dough to center and shape into a ball once again. Cover with plastic wrap and let rise a second time until doubled, about 45 minutes to 1 hour. Punch risen dough down in center a second time. Transfer to a lightly floured board and knead briefly. Reshape into a ball. Cover with towel and let dough rest for at least 30 minutes so gluten will relax and rolling will be easier. Dough is now ready to be rolled, topped, and cooked.

PER SLICE: Cal. 71   Chol. 0 mg
               Fat 1 gm   Sod. 31 mg

~~~~~~

Garlic and Fresh Rosemary Focaccia

[Focaccia di Aglio e Rosmarino]

MAKES ONE FOCACCIA YIELDING 24 SLICES

This focaccia is very appealing for anyone who loves the flavor of garlic.

1 recipe Focaccia Dough (page 169)

⅓ cup thinly sliced garlic (paper-thin)

⅓ cup Beef Broth, preferably homemade (page 4), or defatted low-sodium canned

2 tablespoons extra virgin olive oil

½ teaspoon coarse salt

¾ teaspoon crushed red pepper flakes

2 tablespoons minced fresh rosemary

1. Prepare focaccia dough.
2. Adjust oven rack one shelf up from bottom of oven and preheat to 475°F. for 30 minutes.
3. In a 10-inch nonstick skillet, cook garlic in beef broth over low heat until no liquid is left in bottom of pan, about 5 minutes.
4. Lightly grease a 10 × 15-inch jelly roll pan with cooking spray.
5. Place dough on well-floured work surface. With the palms of your hands, flatten dough into a rectangular shape. Flip dough over. Using a rolling pin, shape dough into a rectangle about 10 × 15 inches, turning and stretching it gently as you roll. Place on prepared pan. With your fingertips, make dimples in dough, leaving indentations that are as deep as ½ inch. Lightly brush surface with oil. Distribute garlic evenly over surface. Sprinkle with salt, pepper flakes, and rosemary.
6. Bake until edges are lightly golden and bottom crust is crisp, about 30 minutes. Transfer to cutting board, cool slightly, slice into squares, and serve.

PER SLICE: Cal. 79   Chol. 0 mg
            Fat 2 gm   Sod. 62 mg

~~~~~~

Onion and
Fresh Sage Focaccia

[Focaccia di Cipolla e Salvia]

MAKES ONE FOCACCIA YIELDING 24 SLICES

The secret to keeping the fat down in this focaccia is cooking the onions in chicken broth until very lightly golden. This is a savory accompaniment to Winter Vegetable Soup (page 15).

1 recipe Focaccia Dough (page 169)

2 cups thinly sliced Spanish onion

½ cup Chicken Broth, preferably homemade (page 5), or defatted low-sodium canned

2 tablespoons extra virgin olive oil

½ teaspoon coarse salt

¾ teaspoon freshly milled black pepper

3 tablespoons coarsely chopped fresh sage

1. Prepare focaccia dough.
2. Adjust oven rack one shelf up from bottom of oven and preheat to 475°F. for 30 minutes.
3. In a 10-inch nonstick skillet, cook onions in chicken broth over medium heat until onions just start to turn golden and no liquid is left in bottom of pan, about 8 minutes.
4. Lightly grease a 10 × 15-inch jelly roll pan with cooking spray.
5. Place dough on well-floured work surface. With the palms of your hands, flatten dough into a rectangular shape. Flip dough over. Using a rolling pin, shape dough into a rectangle about 10 × 15 inches, turning and stretching it gently as you roll. Place on prepared pan. With your fingertips, make dimples in dough, leaving indentations that are as deep as ½ inch. Lightly brush surface with oil. Distribute onion evenly over surface. Sprinkle with salt, pepper, and sage.

6. Bake until edges are lightly golden and bottom crust is crisp, about 30 minutes. Transfer to cutting board, cool slightly, slice into squares, and serve.

PER SLICE: Cal. 87   Chol. 0 mg
               Fat 2 gm   Sod. 64 mg

Desserts

Introduction

While desserts were never considered the highlight of an Italian menu, most of us do enjoy something sweet after a meal.

Traditionally, the simplest dessert to complement any great Italian meal is a platter of fresh fruit picked at the peak of the season, served with a cup of dark roasted espresso. Fruit could be laced with liqueurs, macerated or poached with wines, and served either at the end of the meal or as a late afternoon snack. Historically, the main meal was served midday. Late in the afternoon, it was not uncommon to find people gathering for a sweet course of tiramisù (which translates to "pick-me-up"), granita, torta, or assorted biscotti.

Lightened interpretations of these family classics designed to add that well-loved sweet touch with a fraction of the fat and calories appear on the following pages.

Apricot Cream

[Crema di Albicocche]

⊞

SERVES 8

Light and nearly effortless to make, this Amaretto-flavored dessert makes a fine conclusion to dinner for anyone who loves apricots.

1 envelope (1 tablespoon) unflavored gelatin
1½ cups 1% low-fat milk
One 6-ounce package dried apricots, preferably Sun-Maid
1½ cups part-skim ricotta cheese

⅓ cup sugar
2 tablespoons Amaretto liqueur
¼ teaspoon almond extract
2 tablespoons plus 2 teaspoons slivered almonds, lightly toasted, for garnish

1. In a small saucepan, combine gelatin with milk. Let stand for 2 minutes to soften. Stir over low heat until gelatin is dissolved, about 3 minutes. Transfer to small bowl and place in refrigerator until the mixture sets to the consistency of yogurt, about 90 minutes.
2. Blanch apricots in 2 cups hot water for 30 seconds. Drain in strainer, let cool, blot dry, and coarsely chop; set aside.
3. In electric mixer fitted with whip attachment, beat ricotta, sugar, Amaretto, and almond extract on medium speed until very smooth, about 2 minutes. Transfer to deep bowl and stir in chopped apricots. Refrigerate until needed.
4. In clean dry bowl of electric mixer fitted with whip attachment, place milk-gelatin mixture. Whip on high speed until it is quadrupled in volume and the consistency of beaten egg whites, about 5 to 8 minutes. With rubber spatula, fold gently into ricotta mixture. Ladle into eight 8-ounce wine goblets. Place in refrigerator and chill for 2 hours. (Dessert can be made up to 4 hours before serving.) Garnish each portion with 1 teaspoon slivered almonds just before serving.

PER SERVING: Cal. 190   Chol. 16 mg
              Fat 5 gm   Sod. 83 mg

Cappuccino Mousse

[Cappuccino Semifreddo]

SERVES 8

Your guests will feel quite pampered when served this velvety, rich-tasting mousse. Don't tell them the calorie count until they have finished the last spoonful!

1	envelope (1 tablespoon) unflavored gelatin	2	tablespoons Kahlúa (coffee liqueur)
1½	cups 1% low-fat milk	One	8-ounce package light cream cheese (Neufchâtel), at room temperature
1	tablespoon instant espresso powder		
½	cup hot water	4	teaspoons grated dark semisweet chocolate, for garnish
½	cup sugar		

1. In a small saucepan, combine gelatin and milk. Let stand for 2 minutes to soften. Stir over low heat until gelatin is dissolved, about 3 minutes. Transfer to small bowl and place in refrigerator until mixture sets to the consistency of yogurt, about 90 minutes.
2. In a 2-cup glass measuring cup, dissolve espresso powder in hot water. Add sugar and stir to dissolve. Let cool to room temperature and stir in coffee liqueur.
3. In electric mixer fitted with whip attachment, beat cream cheese on medium speed until smooth. Add coffee mixture and beat on low speed until blended. Stop machine and scrape inside of bowl with rubber spatula. Beat on medium speed until cream cheese is completely dissolved into coffee mixture. Transfer to a large deep bowl.
4. In clean dry bowl of electric mixer fitted with whip attachment, place milk-gelatin mixture. Whip on high speed until it is quadrupled in volume and the consistency of well-beaten egg whites, about 5 minutes. Whisk ⅓ of the beaten milk mixture into coffee mixture. With rubber spatula, fold remaining milk mixture into coffee mixture. Ladle into eight 8-ounce wine goblets and refrig-

erate until set, about 2 hours. (Dessert can be made one day ahead, covered with plastic wrap, and refrigerated until needed.) Garnish each portion with ½ teaspoon grated chocolate just before serving.

PER SERVING: Cal. 150   Chol. 17 mg
                 Fat 6 gm   Sod. 184 mg

Coffee Granita
[Granita di Caffe]

SERVES 4

Traditionally, granita is frozen until it's quite solid, then shaved into dessert dishes at serving time, which produces a very grainy frozen dessert. Whirling in the food processor before serving makes for a much smoother presentation.

2 cups double-strength espresso   ½ cup sugar
   coffee or ¼ cup instant
   espresso powder dissolved
   in 2 cups hot water

1. Stir hot coffee and sugar until the sugar dissolves. Cool to room temperature. Pour into a plastic 16-cube ice cube tray and freeze for 5 hours or overnight.
2. When ready to serve, pop cubes out into a low wide bowl. Place 8 cubes in food processor fitted with metal blade and process until smooth, about 30 seconds. Spoon into two 8-ounce wine goblets and place in freezer to keep well chilled while repeating with remaining cubes.

PER SERVING: Cal. 103   Chol. 0 mg
                 Fat .01gm   Sod. 1 mg

Nectarines in White Wine Syrup

[Pesche Noce con Sciroppo di Vino]

SERVES 4

A very sophisticated dessert for the summer months when well-ripened unblemished nectarines are in season.

½ cup fruity white wine (Chardonnay)

½ cup strained fresh orange juice

1½ tablespoons sugar

1½ tablespoons grated rind of navel orange

¼ teaspoon coarsely ground cinnamon (see Note)

4 large unblemished well-ripened nectarines (about 1¼ pounds), washed, dried, halved, pitted, and sliced lengthwise into ½-inch strips

½ cup fresh raspberries

1. Combine wine, orange juice, sugar, orange rind, and cinnamon in a small saucepan. Bring to a boil over medium heat and cook, stirring constantly, until sugar is dissolved. Transfer to a deep bowl and cool to room temperature.
2. Combine nectarines with wine mixture and stir gently. Cover with plastic wrap and refrigerate for at least 2 hours.
3. Using a slotted spoon, transfer nectarines to four 8-ounce wine-glasses. Spoon about 1 tablespoon of wine syrup over each. Arrange fresh raspberries on top and serve.

Note: To grind cinnamon, break off about a 1-inch piece of cinnamon stick and either grind with a mortar and pestle or in a small electric minimincer. The powdered variety will make the wine syrup cloudy.

PER SERVING: Cal. 126   Chol. 0 mg
Fat .73 gm   Sod. 2 mg

Poached Pears in Red Wine

[Peri Affogati in Vino]

SERVES 6

Poached pears are always a lovely dessert during late fall and winter when the Bosc variety is prevalent. The peppercorns in the poaching liquid give this dessert its spicy flavor.

1¾ cups Cabernet Sauvignon	1½ tablespoons strained fresh
¾ cup water	lemon juice
⅓ cup sugar	One 3-inch cinnamon stick
2 tablespoons grated	14 whole black peppercorns
lemon rind	3 large well-ripened Bosc
	pears (1½ pounds)

1. In a deep 12-inch nonaluminum skillet, combine all of the ingredients except pears. Slowly bring liquid to a boil over medium-high heat. Turn heat to low, cover pan, and cook poaching liquid until sugar is completely dissolved, about 4 minutes, while preparing pears.

2. Remove core and stem from each pear, peel fruit with a vegetable peeler, and cut pears in half lengthwise. Using a melon baller, scoop out and remove center core. Cut away the fibrous line leading from the core to stem end.

3. Reduce heat so that poaching liquid is barely simmering. Place pears in liquid, cut sides down. Partially cover and let pears poach for about 12 minutes. Gently turn pears every 5 minutes and continue cooking, uncovered, basting frequently, until pears are tender when tested with a cake tester, about 20 minutes. Remove from heat, cover pan, and let pears cool to room temperature in poaching liquid. Using a slotted spoon, remove pears to a low wide bowl.

4. Bring poaching liquid to a slow boil and cook until it is slightly

thickened, about 5 minutes. Strain it over pears, cover, and refrigerate for at least 1 hour until chilled.

5. When ready to serve, transfer each pear half to a serving plate, cut side down. Starting ½ inch from top, cut pear halves lengthwise at ¼-inch intervals and press gently to fan out slices. Spoon a little of the poaching liquid over each and serve.

PER SERVING: Cal. 112   Chol. 0 mg
                Fat .41 gm   Sod. 4 mg

Peaches in Chianti

[Pesche con Vino Rosso]

SERVES 4

This was always a favorite with my grandfather Nono Donato. Select well-ripened cling variety of peaches that are tinged with a little red. After soaking in the wine, the peaches will remain quite firm and crunchy when served.

4 large ripe peaches (about 2 pounds)	1 cup Chianti (or any dry red wine)
1½ tablespoons sugar	

1. Gently drop peaches into 6 cups boiling water to blanch for 2 minutes. Transfer to a strainer and rinse under cold water. When cool enough to handle, peel skins, cut peaches in half, discard stones, and slice peaches lengthwise into ½-inch wedges.
2. Place sliced peaches in bowl, preferably glass, sprinkle with sugar, mix, and let stand at room temperature 10 minutes until sugar is dissolved. Add red wine and let sit at room temperature to macerate for 1 hour.
3. When ready to serve, divide into individual dishes and spoon sweetened wine over each.

PER SERVING: Cal. 135   Chol. 0 mg
                Fat .15 gm   Sod. 3 mg

~~~~~~

Prune and Raisin Cake

[Torta di Prune e Uvetta]

▦

SERVES 12

This dense and delicious Sicilian-style cake accented with anise flavoring is a good substitute for fruit cake.

½ cup (about 12) pitted prunes, well packed

3 tablespoons boiling water

⅔ cup strained fresh orange juice

½ cup golden raisins

2 teaspoons anise seed

1 tablespoon grated orange rind

1 large egg, well beaten

2 teaspoons pure vanilla extract

1⅓ cups bleached all-purpose flour

½ cup sugar

1 teaspoon baking powder

½ teaspoon baking soda

1 tablespoon confectioners' sugar, for garnish

1. Adjust oven rack to center of oven and preheat to 350°F. Lightly grease a 10-inch round cake pan 2 inches deep with vegetable cooking spray and dust lightly with flour. Line bottom of pan with parchment paper; set aside.
2. Place prunes in a small bowl, pour boiling water over, and let stand 3 minutes to soften. Transfer prunes and liquid to food processor and process until prunes are finely minced, about 30 seconds; transfer to small bowl.
3. Place orange juice, raisins, and anise seed in a medium deep bowl. Let stand until raisins are slightly softened, about 5 minutes. Stir in minced prunes, orange rind, beaten egg, and vanilla extract.
4. In a large deep bowl, sift together flour, sugar, baking powder, and baking soda. Stir raisin mixture into dry ingredients until thoroughly blended. Turn batter into prepared pan.
5. Bake in preheated oven until cake is lightly golden and a wooden toothpick inserted in center comes out clean, about 30 minutes. Let cake cool in pan on wire rack for 10 minutes. Invert onto wire rack, remove pan, peel off parchment paper, and invert again

onto second rack. Let cake cool completely before transferring to cake plate. (Cake can be made 1 day in advance. Cover loosely with foil and leave at room temperature.) Dust with confectioners' sugar before serving.

PER SERVING: Cal. 137   Chol. 17 mg
Fat .74 gm   Sod. 76 mg

Raspberry Tiramisù

[Tiramisù con Lampone]

SERVES 12

Both dieters and nondieters will revel in this reformed, updated version of tiramisù. If raspberries are unavailable, substitute 1 cup thinly sliced strawberries for filling and border on top with 1 cup halved strawberries.

½ cup boiling water
1 tablespoon instant espresso powder or instant coffee powder
2 tablespoons sugar
2 tablespoons Cognac or brandy
1½ packages (12 ounces) light cream cheese (Neufchâtel), at room temperature

½ cup part-skim ricotta cheese
½ cup confectioners' sugar
2 teaspoons pure vanilla extract
Two 3-ounce packages ladyfingers
1¾ cups fresh raspberries
1½ tablespoons coarsely grated bittersweet chocolate

1. In a glass measuring cup, combine boiling water, coffee powder, and sugar. Let cool a little and stir in Cognac.
2. In food processor, place cream cheese, ricotta cheese, confectioners' sugar, and vanilla extract. Process until blended, about 30 seconds; transfer to medium-size bowl.

3. Arrange 1 package of split ladyfingers cut sides up in a 9 × 9 × 2-inch square glass baking dish. Brush ladyfingers with half of the coffee mixture. Spread half of the cheese mixture over ladyfingers. Arrange 1¼ cups raspberries in rows spaced ½ inch apart over cheese mixture. Repeat with remaining ladyfingers, coffee mixture, and cheese mixture. Sprinkle grated chocolate over surface. Make an outside border of the remaining ½ cup raspberries, spacing them about 1 inch apart. Cover with plastic wrap and refrigerate until set, about 3 hours or overnight. Cut into squares and serve.

PER SERVING: Cal. 176   Chol. 68 mg
              Fat 7 gm   Sod. 183 mg

Ricotta Cheesecake

[Torta di Ricotta]

SERVES 12

This is a calorie-trimmed version of the traditional Italian cheesecake. Unlike most cheesecakes, which require refrigeration overnight, this one can be served the same day it is made.

One 15-ounce container part-skim ricotta cheese

¾ cup graham cracker crumbs (12 squares)

One 8-ounce package light cream cheese (Neufchâtel), at room temperature

¼ cup all-purpose flour

⅓ cup sugar

1 large egg, at room temperature

3 large egg whites, at room temperature

2 teaspoons pure vanilla extract

2 teaspoons grated orange rind

1 pint strawberries, washed, hulled, dried, and sliced in half lengthwise

⅓ cup apricot preserves, heated and strained

1. Place ricotta in strainer set over a bowl and let drain at room temperature for 1 hour.
2. Adjust oven rack to center of oven and preheat to 300°F. Lightly grease bottom and sides of a 9-inch springform pan with solid vegetable shortening. Press crumbs into bottom of prepared pan; set aside.
3. In an electric mixer, beat ricotta and cream cheese on medium speed until smooth, about 1 minute. Stop mixer and scrape down beaters and inside of bowl with rubber spatula. Add flour and sugar; beat on medium speed until blended, about 30 seconds. Add whole egg and beat on low speed until blended, about 30 seconds. Add egg whites and beat another 30 seconds until blended. Blend in vanilla extract and orange rind. Turn batter into prepared pan and set pan on a cookie sheet to catch any leakage while baking.
4. Bake in preheated oven until filling is barely set in center when lightly touched, about 45 minutes. Turn oven off and leave cake in oven with door closed for an additional 20 minutes. Set cake on wire rack until completely cool. (Cake can be served the same day it is baked or covered with plastic wrap and refrigerated overnight.)
5. Up to 3 hours before serving, run knife around inside of pan and remove springform. Place cake on platter with folded piece of dampened paper towel in center to prevent bottom of pan from sliding when slicing. Starting from outside edge of cake, arrange strawberries, cut sides down, in overlapping concentric circles. Brush with apricot glaze and refrigerate. Remove from refrigerator ½ hour before serving.

PER SERVING: Cal. 194   Chol. 38 mg
              Fat 7 gm   Sod. 216 mg

Roasted Chestnuts

[Arrosto di Castagne]

SERVES 6

A family favorite, for snacking or serving after dinner in late fall when chestnuts are in season. After roasting, the chestnuts are transferred to a deep pot and soaked with wine until wine is completely absorbed. The shells soften a little and are a breeze to peel while the chestnuts remain moist.

1 pound fresh chestnuts   ½ cup dry white wine

1. Adjust oven rack to upper portion of oven and preheat to 450°F.
2. Using the tip of a small paring knife, cut an X on the rounded side of each chestnut about ¼ inch deep. Place chestnuts in a 3-quart saucepan and cover with water. Bring to a boil and cook just until the shells start to open, about 5 minutes. Thoroughly drain and place on a cookie sheet with cut sides up.
3. Bake in preheated oven until chestnuts are soft inside their shells, about 20 to 30 minutes, depending on size. Test by peeling one and tasting. Transfer roasted chestnuts to a 3-quart saucepan and pour wine over them. Cover with lid and shake pot vigorously two or three times. Leave covered until all the wine is absorbed into chestnuts, about 15 minutes. Transfer to a basket and serve warm.

PER SERVING: Cal. 221   Chol. 0 mg
              Fat 2 gm   Sod. 20 mg

Strawberries with Orange Liqueur

[Fragole con Liquore Arancia]

▨

SERVES 4

A very impressive low-calorie dessert that can be prepared in a matter of minutes.

1 quart strawberries, washed, well drained, hulled, and halved lengthwise	2 tablespoons superfine sugar
⅓ cup strained fresh orange juice	2 teaspoons freshly grated orange rind
2 tablespoons Grand Marnier liqueur	4 short sprigs fresh mint, for garnish

1. Place strawberries in a medium-size bowl.
2. Place juice, liqueur, and sugar in a small bowl. Stir the mixture with a whisk until sugar is dissolved. Pour mixture over strawberries. Add orange rind and gently stir to combine. Cover with plastic wrap and chill for 1 hour.
3. Ladle strawberry mixture into four 8-ounce wineglasses. Garnish each with a sprig of mint and serve.

PER SERVING: Cal. 103   Chol. 0 mg
               Fat .63 gm   Sod. 2 mg

~~~~~~

Stuffed Baked Apples

[Mele Infornate]

SERVES 6

Like baked apples? Try this simple method of preparation, but remember to keep basting them after they come out of the oven so they will be completely glazed when served.

6 medium-size baking apples, preferably Rome (about 2½ pounds)
½ cup dark raisins
⅓ cup lightly packed light brown sugar
1 teaspoon ground cinnamon

2 tablespoons dark rum or brandy
½ cup dark corn syrup
1 teaspoon pure vanilla extract
1 teaspoon freshly ground nutmeg
1½ cups unsweetened apple juice

1. Adjust oven rack to center of oven and preheat to 350°F.
2. Using a melon baller, core apples from stem end without cutting through to bottom. Using a vegetable peeler, peel off skin about halfway down each apple.
3. In a small bowl, combine raisins, brown sugar, cinnamon, and rum. Fill cavity of each apple with raisin mixture. Place apples in a 9 × 13 × 2-inch baking dish.
4. In a small bowl, combine dark corn syrup with vanilla. Spoon mixture over apples; sprinkle each with nutmeg.
5. Pour apple juice into bottom of baking dish. Place in oven and bake apples for 20 minutes. Using a bulb-type baster, baste apples with pan juices. Continue baking and basting every 10 minutes until apples are extremely tender when tested with a cake tester, about 45 minutes. Remove from oven and keep basting with pan juices every 5 minutes until apples are well coated with glaze. Serve warm or at room temperature with a little glaze over each.

PER SERVING: Cal. 218   Chol. 0 mg
Fat .64 gm   Sod. 31 mg

Watermelon Granita

[Granita di Melone]

✦

SERVES 6

Select bright-red fleshed watermelon for this refreshing dessert. Spooning blueberries on top of the granita makes a particularly appealing and colorful combination.

4 cups well-packed diced watermelon (1-inch dice), seeds removed

⅓ cup superfine sugar

3 tablespoons strained fresh lemon juice

¾ cup blueberries, stems removed, washed, and blotted dry

6 sprigs fresh mint, for garnish

1. Place watermelon in food processor fitted with metal blade. Process to a smooth purée, about 15 to 20 seconds. Transfer to deep bowl; stir in sugar and juice. Pour mixture into a 9 × 13 × 2-inch baking pan and place in freezer. Freeze until granita is frozen around edges and center is still slushy, about 1 hour. Using fork, stir mixture well, breaking up frozen pieces around inside edge of pan. Continue freezing, stirring every half hour, until granita is consistency of shaved ice, about 3½ hours.

2. To serve, scoop granita out with an ice cream scoop or wide metal spoon into six 8-ounce wineglasses. Spoon 2 tablespoons blueberries over each portion, garnish with mint, and serve.

PER SERVING: Cal. 88   Chol. 0 mg
              Fat .51 gm   Sod. 3 mg

Cookies

Introduction

My father-in-law, Vincenzo Casale, was an Italian pastry chef of the first order. After his retirement, I would assist him in the kitchen baking many of his favorite cookies. Although he was working in a standard home kitchen, he continued to work on a large scale and insisted upon using the same amounts of ingredients he had used at the bakery. It became my challenge in adapting his classic recipes not only to scale down these measurements but also to reduce the amounts of shortening, sugar, and nuts so abundant in his delicacies without sacrificing taste and flavor.

The following collection of cookies and biscotti can be served as an accompaniment to the fruit desserts or granita. They make an excellent low-fat snack at any time, and are ideal served with a Tuscan sweet wine called Vin Santo or alongside a cup of coffee or tea.

Almond Cookies

[Quaresimale]

MAKES 4 DOZEN COOKIES

With the nutty sweetness of toasted almonds and just a hint of cinnamon, these cookies are a delightful snack or perfect when served with Coffee Granita (page 179). A favorite with family, friends, and students.

1 cup whole almonds with skins on	2 tablespoons extra light olive oil
¾ cup sugar	1 large egg
1 cup bleached all-purpose flour	1 teaspoon pure vanilla extract
1 teaspoon ground cinnamon	
½ teaspoon baking powder	1 large egg white, lightly beaten
½ teaspoon baking soda	

1. Adjust oven rack to center of oven and preheat to 375°F. Place almonds on small cookie sheet and toast until golden brown, about 10 minutes. Transfer almonds to bowl of electric mixer.
2. Raise oven temperature to 425°F. Line a 14 × 16-inch cookie sheet with parchment paper; set aside.
3. Add sugar, flour, cinnamon, baking powder, and baking soda to almonds. Mix on low speed until ingredients are combined. Add oil and mix on low speed until blended.
4. In a small bowl, whisk together egg and vanilla; add to batter. Run machine on low speed until dough comes together in a slightly sticky mass and the nuts break up a little, about 1½ minutes. Turn dough out onto a clean, dry work surface and divide in half. Shape into 2 ropes approximately 12 inches long. Place 4 inches apart on prepared pan. With fingertips, flatten each into a log ½ inch thick, 2 inches wide, and 14 inches long. Brush logs with lightly beaten egg white.
5. Bake in preheated oven until golden and slightly firm to the touch, about 15 to 20 minutes. Place cookie sheet on wire rack and let cool for 5 minutes. With a serrated knife, cut logs crosswise into

~~~~~~

½-inch slices. Transfer cookies to wire rack and cool thoroughly. They will become crisp when cooled. Cookies can be stored in a tin lined with wax paper for 4 weeks.

PER COOKIE: Cal. 43   Chol. 4 mg
            Fat 2 gm   Sod. 16 mg

Anise- and Orange-Flavored Biscuits

[Biscotti all' Anice e Aranci]

▦

MAKES 4 DOZEN COOKIES

Grated orange rind enlivens the flavor of these anise-flavored biscotti. They are suberb any time of day.

2 cups bleached all-purpose flour
1½ teaspoons baking powder
⅛ teaspoon salt
1½ teaspoons anise seed
1 tablespoon grated rind of navel orange
½ cup sugar

2 tablespoons extra light olive oil
1 large egg
1 large egg white
1½ teaspoons pure vanilla extract
1 large egg white, lightly beaten

1. Adjust oven rack to center of oven and preheat to 350°F. Line a 14 × 16-inch cookie sheet with parchment paper; set aside.
2. Place flour, baking powder, salt, anise seed, and orange rind in a medium-size bowl. Stir to combine well.
3. Place sugar, oil, whole egg, 1 egg white, and vanilla in bowl of electric mixer. Beat on medium speed for 1 minute.
4. Add flour mixture and run machine on low speed until dough comes together in a sticky mass, about 1 minute.

5. Turn the dough out onto a well floured work surface and divide in half. With lightly floured hands, shape into 2 ropes approximately 13 inches long. Place 4 inches apart on prepared pan. With fingertips, lightly flatten each into a log ½ inch high, 2 inches wide, and 14 inches long. Brush logs with lightly beaten egg white.

6. Bake in preheated oven until lightly golden, about 20 minutes. Place cookie sheet on wire rack to cool for 5 minutes. Raise oven temperature to 375°F. Transfer logs to cutting board; discard parchment paper. With a serrated knife, cut logs diagonally into ½-inch slices. Place slices cut side down on baking pan and return to oven. Bake until slightly toasted, about 10 minutes. Transfer biscotti to wire rack and cool completely. Biscotti can be stored in a tin lined with wax paper for 2 weeks.

PER COOKIE: Cal. 35   Chol. 4 mg
                Fat .74 gm   Sod. 23 mg

Chocolate
Hazelnut Biscuits

[Biscotti di Cioccolato e Nocciole]

MAKES 4 DOZEN COOKIES

Dutch process cocoa and toasted hazelnuts contribute a double flavor impact to this enticing variation. A favorite with my editor, Joelle Delbourgo.

⅔ cup hazelnuts	1 teaspoon baking powder
1¾ cups bleached all-purpose flour	⅛ teaspoon salt
	2 tablespoons extra light olive oil
¾ cup sugar	
⅓ cup unsweetened Dutch process cocoa	3 large egg whites
	1½ teaspoons pure vanilla extract
1 tablespoon instant espresso coffee powder	1 egg white, lightly beaten

1. Adjust oven rack to center of oven and preheat to 350°F.
2. Place hazelnuts on small cookie sheet and toast until nuts are a dark golden color and skins blister, about 10 minutes. Place nuts in a dish towel and rub to remove skins. Transfer nuts to bowl of electric mixer.
3. Line a 14 × 16-inch cookie sheet with parchment paper; set aside.
4. Add flour, sugar, cocoa, coffee powder, baking powder, and salt to hazelnuts. Mix on low speed until ingredients are combined. Add oil and mix on low speed until blended.
5. In a small bowl, whisk together 3 egg whites and vanilla; add to batter. Run machine on low speed until dough comes together in a slightly sticky mass and the nuts break up a little, about 1½ minutes. Turn dough out onto a clean, dry work surface and divide in half. Shape into 2 ropes approximately 12 inches long. Place ropes 4 inches apart on prepared pan. With fingertips, flatten each into a log ½ inch thick, 2 inches wide, and 14 inches long. Brush logs with lightly beaten egg white.

~~~~~~

6. Bake in preheated 350°F. oven until firm to the touch, about 20 minutes. Place cookie sheet on wire rack to cool for 5 minutes. Lower oven temperature to 300°F. Transfer logs to cutting board; discard parchment paper. With a serrated knife, cut logs diagonally into ½-inch slices. Place slices cut side down on baking pan and return to oven. Bake until dry to the touch, about 15 minutes. Transfer biscotti to wire rack and cool completely. Biscotti can be stored in a tin lined with wax paper for 3 weeks.

PER COOKIE: Cal. 46   Chol. 0 mg
                Fat 1 gm   Sod. 28 mg

Hazelnut Meringue Cookies

[Meringa di Nocciole]

MAKES 3 DOZEN COOKIES

These chewy, nutty meringue cookies are a favorite with my husband, John.

½ cup hazelnuts
½ cup sugar
2½ teaspoons cornstarch
3 large egg whites, at room temperature

Pinch of salt
⅛ teaspoon cream of tartar
½ teaspoon pure vanilla extract
¼ teaspoon almond extract

1. Adjust oven rack to center of oven and preheat to 350°F. Place hazelnuts on small cookie sheet and toast until nuts are a dark golden color and skins blister, about 10 minutes. Place nuts in a dish towel and rub to remove skins; let nuts cool to room temperature.

2. Lower oven temperature to 225°F. Line a 14 × 16-inch cookie sheet with parchment paper; set aside.

3. Place nuts in food processor or blender with 2 tablespoons sugar; process until finely ground. Transfer to a small bowl and combine with cornstarch; set aside.

4. Place egg whites and salt in the bowl of an electric mixer fitted with whip attachment. Beat until frothy, add the cream of tartar, and beat until whites hold soft peaks. Beat in the remaining sugar, 1 tablespoon at a time, and continue to beat the meringue until it holds stiff peaks. Add the vanilla and almond extract and beat the meringue for 1 minute. With a rubber spatula, fold in ¼ of the nut mixture. Thoroughly fold in remaining nut mixture, ¼ at a time.

5. Spoon rounded tablespoons of the meringue onto prepared cookie sheet about 1½ inches apart. Bake until very lightly colored and firm to the touch, about 35 to 40 minutes. Turn oven off and let the cookies dry in the oven for at least 3 hours. Peel cookies off parchment. Cookies can be stored in a tin lined with wax paper for 1 week.

PER COOKIE: Cal. 23   Chol. 0 mg
               Fat 1 gm   Sod. 8 mg

Honey-Walnut Cinnamon Biscuits

[Biscotti alla Vincenzo]

MAKES 5 DOZEN COOKIES

These twice-baked classical Italian dunking biscuits are a perfect accent with a cup of espresso or cappuccino.

1¼ cups walnuts

2 cups bleached all-purpose flour

½ cup well-packed light brown sugar

½ teaspoon baking powder

½ teaspoon baking soda

1 teaspoon ground cinnamon

⅓ cup honey

⅓ cup water

1. Adjust oven rack to center of oven and preheat to 350°F.
2. Place walnuts on small cookie sheet and toast until lightly colored, about 7 minutes. Transfer walnuts to bowl of electric mixer.
3. Line a 14 × 16-inch cookie sheet with parchment paper; set aside.
4. Add flour, brown sugar, baking powder, baking soda, and cinnamon to walnuts. Mix on low speed until ingredients are combined. Add honey and water and run machine on low speed until dough comes together in a sticky mass and nuts break up a little, about 1 minute. Turn dough out onto a lightly floured work surface and divide into thirds. With lightly floured hands, shape into 3 ropes approximately 11 inches long. Place 2½ inches apart on prepared pan. With fingertips, flatten each into a log ½ inch thick, 2 inches wide, and 12½ inches long.
5. Bake in preheated 350°F. oven until a light golden color and firm to the touch, about 20 minutes. Place cookie sheet on wire rack to cool for 5 minutes. Transfer logs to cutting board; discard parchment paper. With a serrated knife, cut logs diagonally into ½-inch slices. Place slices cut side down on baking pan and return

to oven. Bake until golden brown, about 12 to 15 minutes. Transfer biscotti to wire rack and cool completely. Biscotti can be stored in a tin lined with wax paper for 3 weeks.

PER COOKIE: Cal. 44   Chol. 0 mg
              Fat 2 gm   Sod. 11 mg

Ladyfingers
[Savoiardi]

MAKES 2½ DOZEN COOKIES

Savoiardi are one of the most basic Italian cookies. Excellent on their own as a light, and low-calorie cookie, or a perfect accompaniment to Nectarines in Wine Syrup (page 180).

1 cup bleached all-purpose flour	½ cup sugar
1 teaspoon baking powder	Pinch of salt
3 large eggs, separated, at room temperature	1 egg white, lightly beaten
2 teaspoons pure vanilla extract	2 tablespoons sifted confectioners' sugar, for dusting

1. Line two 14 × 16-inch cookie sheets with parchment paper. Fit a 12-inch pastry bag with a ½-inch plain tube. Adjust oven rack to center of oven and preheat to 400°F.
2. On a piece of wax paper, sift together flour and baking powder; set aside.
3. Place egg yolks, vanilla, and ¼ cup sugar in the bowl of an electric mixer fitted with whip attachment. Beat mixture on medium-high speed until light, thick, and lemon-colored, about 5 to 7 minutes. Transfer mixture to another bowl.
4. In a clean, dry bowl of the electric mixer fitted with clean whip attachment, place egg whites and pinch of salt; beat on medium

speed until foamy. Turn speed to high and beat in the remaining ¼ cup sugar gradually until the whites hold a shiny peak. Using a rubber spatula, fold the yolk mixture into the beaten whites. In two batches fold the flour mixture into the egg mixture.

5. Fill the pastry bag with half of the batter and pipe strips 2½ inches long by 1 inch wide about 1 inch apart onto prepared pan. Lightly brush strips with beaten egg white.

6. Bake until lightly golden and firm to the touch, about 10 to 12 minutes. Prepare second batch while first batch is baking. Carefully slide the whole sheet of parchment onto wire rack. Thoroughly cool cookies on rack. Peel ladyfingers off parchment paper. Ladyfingers can be stored in a tin lined with wax paper between layers for 1 week. Dust with confectioners' sugar just before serving.

PER COOKIE: Cal. 34   Chol. 20 mg
             Fat .49 gm Sod. 23 mg

Spiced Fruit Biscuits

[Biscotti di Frutti]

MAKES 5½ DOZEN COOKIES

The macerated dried fruits lend a chewy bite to these crunchy biscuits. The flavor improves when they are stored in a tin for a few days.

½ cup diced pitted prunes (¼-inch dice)

½ cup stemmed, diced, dried Calimyrna figs (¼-inch dice)

½ cup chopped golden raisins

¼ cup Cognac or brandy

2 cups bleached all-purpose flour

⅔ cup sugar

1 teaspoon baking powder

1 teaspoon baking soda

1 teaspoon freshly grated nutmeg

1 tablespoon finely grated lemon rind

1 large egg

2 large egg whites

1½ teaspoons pure lemon extract

1 large egg white, lightly beaten

1. Adjust oven rack to center of oven and preheat to 350°F. Line a 14 × 16-inch cookie sheet with parchment paper; set aside.
2. Place prunes, figs, and raisins in a medium-size bowl. Stir in Cognac and set aside to macerate for 15 minutes.
3. Place flour, sugar, baking powder, baking soda, nutmeg, and lemon rind in bowl of electric mixer. Run machine on low speed to combine, about 1 minute.
4. In a small bowl, whisk together whole egg, 2 egg whites, and lemon extract. Add to flour mixture and run machine on medium speed until mixture is the consistency of coarse crumbs. Add macerated fruit and run machine on low speed until fruit is blended and dough comes together in a sticky mass. Turn dough out onto a well-floured work surface and divide into thirds. With well-floured hands, shape into 3 ropes approximately 12 inches long.

Place 2½ inches apart on prepared pan. With fingertips, flatten each into a log ½ inch thick, 2 inches wide, and 14 inches long. Brush logs with lightly beaten egg white.

5. Bake in preheated oven until golden and firm to the touch, about 20 minutes. Place cookie sheet on wire rack to cool for 5 minutes. Lower oven temperature to 300°F. Transfer logs to cutting board; discard parchment paper. With a serrated knife, cut logs diagonally into ½-inch slices. Stand the slices upright on baking sheet and return to oven. Bake until cut surfaces are dry to the touch, about 25 minutes. Transfer biscotti to wire rack and cool completely. Biscotti can be stored in a tin lined with wax paper for 3 weeks.

PER COOKIE: Cal. 34 Chol. 3 mg
  Fat .12 gm Sod. 23 mg

Index

D

E

F

ABOUT THE AUTHOR

Anne Casale began teaching cooking in 1963 when she founded Annie's Kitchen. She served as president of the New York Association of Cooking Teachers for two terms. She is also a Certified Culinary Professional of the International Association of Culinary Professionals. She has taught in cooking schools throughout the United States and has appeared on numerous television and radio programs. Ms. Casale has worked in sales and marketing and as a lecturer, consultant, and designer for restaurants, gourmet shops, and cooking schools. Ms. Casale is the author of *Italian Family Cooking* and *The Long Life Cookbook*.